# THE LITTLE BOOK

## OF
## TRADING

# *Little Book Big Profits* Series

*In the Little Book Big Profits series, the brightest icons in the financial world write on topics that range from tried-and-true investment strategies to tomorrow's new trends. Each book offers a unique perspective on investing, allowing the reader to pick and choose from the very best in investment advice today.*

*Books in the Little Book Big Profits series include:*

*The Little Book That Still Beats the Market* by Joel Greenblatt
*The Little Book of Value Investing* by Christopher Browne
*The Little Book of Common Sense Investing* by John C. Bogle
*The Little Book That Makes You Rich* by Louis Navellier
*The Little Book That Builds Wealth* by Pat Dorsey
*The Little Book That Saves Your Assets* by David M. Darst
*The Little Book of Bull Moves in Bear Markets* by Peter D. Schiff
*The Little Book of Main Street Money* by Jonathan Clements
*The Little Book of Safe Money* by Jason Zweig
*The Little Book of Behavioral Investing* by James Montier
*The Little Book of Big Dividends* by Charles B. Carlson
*The Little Book of Bulletproof Investing* by Ben Stein and Phil DeMuth
*The Little Book of Commodity Investing* by John R. Stephenson
*The Little Book of Economics* by Greg Ip
*The Little Book of Sideways Markets* by Vitaliy N. Katsenelson
*The Little Book of Currency Trading* by Kathy Lien
*The Little Book of Alternative Investments* by Ben Stein and Phil DeMuth
*The Little Book of Valuation* by Aswath Damodaran
*The Little Book of Trading* by Michael W. Covel

# THE LITTLE BOOK

## OF

# TRADING

*Trend Following Strategy*
*for Big Winnings*

## MICHAEL W. COVEL

WILEY

John Wiley & Sons, Inc.

Published by John Wiley & Sons, Inc., Hoboken, New Jersey.
Published simultaneously in Canada.

For general information on our other products and services or for technical support, please contact our Customer Care Department within the United States at (800) 762-2974, outside the United States at (317) 572-3993 or fax (317) 572-4002.

Wiley also publishes its books in a variety of electronic formats. Some content that appears in print may not be available in electronic books. For more information about Wiley products, visit our web site at www.wiley.com.

*Library of Congress Cataloging-in-Publication Data:*

Covel, Michael.
    The little book of trading : trend following strategy for big winnings / Michael W. Covel.
       p.   cm.—(Little book big profits series)
    ISBN 978-1-118-06350-7 (hardback); 978-1-118-14388-9 (ebk); 978-1-118-14390-2 (ebk); 978-1-118-14389-6 (ebk)
      1. Capitalists and financiers—Case studies.   2. Investments.   3. Investment analysis.   I. Title.
  HG4521.C815  2011
  332.64—dc23                                         2011021445

Printed in the United States of America

10 9 8 7 6 5 4 3 2 1

*This book is dedicated to my grandparents:*
*Wesley Albert Kavaliauskas, Anna Lenore Margis,*
*John Brooke Pruden, Jr., and Mary Margaret Wright*

# Contents

Chapter Nine

Chapter Ten

Chapter Eleven

Chapter Twelve

# Foreword

## Cullen O. Roche

TREND FOLLOWING—IT SOUNDS SO SIMPLE, DOESN'T IT? As Dennis Gartman of the *Gartman Letter* often likes to say: "If the chart is moving from the bottom left to the top right, then I like it." And to the untrained eye, that's all trend following is. It's identifying a trend and riding it. And as the famous saying goes: "The trend is your friend . . . until it ends." And that's where trend following adds so much value. Trend following is not just about identifying great investments. It's about using rules and techniques to manage the risks associated with these investments. What appears to be a very simple strategy at first glance is actually a sophisticated, multidimensional, and vital technique utilized by successful investors all over the world.

I should be clear that I am not a pure trend follower. I use a multistrategy approach primarily due to my belief that no two market environments are ever the same and that markets are highly inefficient. What works in one bull market or bear market will not necessarily work in the next bull or bear market. This is why trading requires a great deal of flexibility and an ability to conform and adapt to new environments. At the core of my work are risk management and the establishment of a systematic approach. Trend following has been absolutely vital in helping me develop the foundation of my investment strategies.

When I graduated from college with a degree in finance I was your typical hungry young investor. But I was lost. And so I did what most investors do, and I began reading the works of those who had already succeeded in the business before me. I printed out every shareholder letter by Warren Buffett, and I read all of the standard books from *A Random Walk Down Wall Street* to *One Up on Wall Street* to *The Intelligent Investor*. And then one day my father gave me Michael Covel's first book *Trend Following*. It didn't look like anything fancy at first glance, but the powerful message conveyed in the book changed the way I viewed investing forever.

You see, trend following isn't just drawing a line on a chart and hoping it continues from the bottom left to the top right. Trend following is about studying the history of market movements, creating a game plan, having rules, learning how to apply those rules, understanding money management, and utilizing a risk management approach. It isn't about using all the failed techniques that the Wall Street establishment has sold to the small investor for so long. Trend following is about thinking outside the box and understanding that the techniques of trend followers are applicable to all markets and all trading strategies. You don't have to agree with the strictly technical analysis aspect of trend following to know that the techniques applied by trend followers are absolutely vital components of any good investor's success story.

One of the more important aspects of trend following is that its users understand the importance of psychology in markets. I like to say that a market is the summation of the decisions of its participants. Markets are inefficient because the participants are inefficient. Thus, the participant with superior emotional control has a decisive advantage. As Michael says:

> Trend trading is not a holy grail. It is not some passing fad or hyped-up secret black box, either. Beyond the mere rules, the human element is

core to the strategy. It takes discipline and emotional control to stick with trend trading through the inevitable market ups and downs. Keep in mind, though, that trend followers expect ups and downs. They are planned for in advance.

This irrationality was on full display in 2008. At the beginning of 2008, before one of the greatest periods of wealth destruction that the world has ever seen, the average Wall Street analyst had a "sell" rating on just 5 percent of the stocks covered, and recommended a "buy" or "hold" on the other 95 percent. Wall Street doesn't prepare you to understand when to sell. You see, Wall Street is always thinking of new ways to get you to buy or hold its new products. If you're a car salesman, it's difficult to make money if you tell everyone who walks onto the lot that they *shouldn't* buy. Trend following closes the loop by not only helping you decipher the right times to buy, but also helping you to manage risks, develop a systematic approach, and identify when to sell. And the results speak for themselves. While the average U.S. equity investor lost 50 percent of his or her money, trend followers crushed the Standard & Poor's 500 in 2008 because they had preestablished risk management structures in their portfolios.

According to an ancient proverb, "failure to plan is planning for failure." Trend followers succeed because they have implemented an investment approach that focuses on risk management and strict adherence to rules. And whereas you don't need to be a trend follower to succeed in the investment world, you certainly need to understand the importance of risk management, the establishment of rules, and planning in advance. If not, you are destined to fail. Michael's *Little Book of Trading* is a must-read guide to help you succeed in the shark-infested waters of the investment world.

—Cullen O. Roche
Founder and CEO, Orsus Investments, LLC
Proprietor of Pragmatic Capitalism

# Introduction

—— ∾ ——

## *A Wake-up Call*

BEN STEIN FAMOUSLY SAID, "IF YOU DIDN'T LOSE A LOT OF money during the Panic of 2008, you were probably doing something wrong." I heard those words and wanted to scream. His view could not be any farther from the truth. People made fortunes in 2008 with solid moneymaking strategies. The winners were not doing anything *wrong*, they just happened to have had the vision to prepare for the unexpected and when the big surprises unfolded—they cleaned up.

Investors have been conditioned for decades to believe that they cannot beat the market. They've been told to buy index funds and mutual funds, listen to CNBC, and trust the government. I have news for you. That does not work. We have all seen one market crash after another for the last decade. But the powers that be keep telling us that the old investing ways are the only way. Deep in our gut we know it's not true. Even if we don't know who the winners are, there are winners in the market, especially in the middle of a crash.

I am going to introduce you to a way of thinking, to a way of making money that is entirely different from what you have been taught. It varies vastly from what you have heard from the brokerage firms, the media, and the government.

First of all, you can leave *fundamental analysis* at the door. A lot of people are taught that fundamental analysis— knowing a company's financial statement backwards and forwards in order to know where to invest, and crunching numbers until you're blue in the face—is the cornerstone of investing. Well, you do not need to know how great the demand will be for the next Apple iPad. You do not need to know how far gold will go up, or down, or why. The only variable to understand, so you can make money, is to know which way the market is trending, and if you are on board, up or down, you go in that direction.

This book is all about trend following trading. Maybe you've never heard of it. Trend following is real simple. Pretend you have no idea which way a market will go or for how long. Trend followers simply say that if Apple is trading at 300, and it starts to go higher, they will buy

Apple. Why would you do this? If Apple is going up you want to be on board. Period. No one knows how high or low Apple may go, but if it goes from 300 to 400 you don't want to miss out—even if 300 feels like too high a price to buy in at. Buying low or cheap is not the goal.

The greatest thing about trend following is that you do not have to know anything about oil. You don't have to know supply and demand for next week or next year. Trend followers don't care. If the market is going up—you buy. After you buy, if it goes the other way and you start to lose money—you get out. How do you know to get out? Trend followers abide by certain universal and timeless rules that go way back. One major rule is accepting when you are wrong in the market and getting out. You need to be willing to lose a small amount of money if the trend does not go your way. The key to keeping that loss as small as possible is admitting defeat. This is how you preserve capital.

Let me break it down. Let's look at Apple again. Assume it is at 300. It goes to 310 and you buy. You hope it will go to 400, but you don't know if it will. So when you buy Apple at 300 you say to yourself, "I am only willing to lose 5 percent of my money" (just an example to bring you in). If you have $100,000 and invest all of it in Apple, then you are willing to lose $5,000 while hoping the trend will go to 400. If Apple starts to go down and you lose $5,000, you get out. That's it. That is trend following in a nutshell. If it doesn't go down, and you don't lose $5,000, you stay along for the ride for as long as it goes.

Another wrinkle to trend following? Not only can you make money when markets go up, you can make money when markets go down. You can go "short" when the trend is down, profiting for as long as markets remain in that direction. This means you can make the same amount of money when Google goes from 600 to 700 as when it goes from 700 to 600.

It's not just stocks. Trend followers apply their "know nothing about a market" to currencies, commodities, bonds, gold, oil—you name it. You do not have to know the name of the market to trade it. Trend traders only care which way the market price is moving so they can get on the train. Or think of yourself as a stowaway on a cruise ship to the islands. Why do you care how the ship gets there? You are already on board. Let someone else worry about the particulars of navigating the ship. Do the top traders really think and act like this? You bet.

Not only did trend following traders make money in 2008, but they've been making it big for decades. Why have most people not heard of this great alternate trading strategy that makes money in bull and bear markets? Why are people not familiar with this moneymaking strategy that performs well during chaos?

One answer: mutual funds.

We have become a world seduced by the idea that you can buy and hold a mutual fund for a lifetime, rewarding you with a huge nest egg when retirement sets in. The vast majority of investors have been sold that pipe dream by the mutual funds themselves. And, they hire serious lobbyists in Washington, D.C. Do you really believe mutual funds are a good idea after a decade of no returns, while simultaneously the owners of mutual funds have made billions?

Let's not dwell there though, since this book doesn't waste much time on bashing the competition. This book is about showing and proving that there *is* a way you can still take your legitimate shot at making the big money. I am going to introduce you to the strategy of trading trends the best way I know how: through the insights of some of the most successful trend following traders alive. Why should you care about these traders?

For one, they are real people performing real trades. They are not CNBC talking heads. They are not academics. They are not politicians. They do not make predictions. They do not make outlandish claims. They simply make money. How do you know for sure they make money?

How do you know they are real? Their audited track records are on file with the United States government (and in Appendix B).

Still asking why this is all relevant to you and your account? I have been teaching, writing, and researching this subject since 1996. The number one reason people fail to adopt trend following trading, or fail to understand it, comes down to education—more specifically, the lack of it.

I have learned that when you expose people to the subject of trend following, introducing readers and students to real winning traders furthers the learning curve by leaps and bounds. Not the shiny PR bios, but real behind the scenes life stories and strategies. If you can go behind the curtain of the greats and even a few newer traders, if you can relate to their upbringing and values, if you can relate to their struggles, you are going to be in a much better position to grasp and utilize trend following strategies for your own account. Better yet, by allowing yourself to *feel* their lives, you will also begin to see that they all have much in common with all of us.

---

**Trading is mental. Doubt me? Want to go some other direction instead? You will be broke in no time.**

Bottom line: I go looking for answers where most people can't or don't know how to go. Digging for trend following trading lessons is my lifeblood.

Plenty of people write books telling you that they know what will happen tomorrow. Do you really want to bet on the words of people who say they know what will happen tomorrow? Doesn't that just feel like a roll of the dice at the craps tables?

Exactly. It is nonsense.

However, I do not want you to take my word. I am going to take you on a trading journey. This journey will have you meeting and learning from eleven traders, all with a similar point of view and trend trading philosophy. These men have literally pulled in billions of profit from the market for decades. They are true trading winners who have shared with me their lessons to money-making success. In turn, I am sharing their wisdom with you.

What are the most common threads among these men and their successes? They were all self-starters not born with silver spoons. They did not start with inheritances (but you could have). They figured out how to win, when everyone said they'd lose. They never quit. As diverse as their stories are, they all make up an inspirational foundation you can use to start making a fortune over the course of your lifetime.

Lastly, and this is important, the lessons that you will learn in this book, the lessons that I will pass along to you, the lessons that these top traders will pass along to you, are rare. These men do not offer extensive insights to the general public. They have trusted me to present the moneymaking story of trend following, and their paths to it, accurately.

I am going to keep the details of the traders' successes out of the chapters to a great extent, and let their trading wisdom shine. But please be aware that these traders are the best of the breed. Many of these men started with nothing and turned nothing into gold. Consider a few details about some of the trading teachers you'll meet:

- **Gary Davis, Jack Forrest,** and **Rick Slaughter** run Sunrise Capital Partners. Their continuous trend following track record extends for 30-plus years.
- **David Harding**, through his firm Winton Capital, has a continuous track record for 20-plus years. Harding has generated a fortune of nearly $1 billion.
- **David Druz** saw his trading account dip to $1,500, 30 years ago. Today, his continuous

track record since 1981 has allowed Druz to make millions, trading comfortably from his office in Hawaii.

- **Kevin Bruce**, who started with $5,000, amassed a fortune of $100 million trading trends over 20-plus years.
- **Paul Mulvaney**, who has a 10-year track record as a trend following trader—gained over 40 percent in the month of October 2008. Yes, the craziest month of the last 30 years, and he killed it.

This is not a complete list. It is a taste to let you see that you are learning from top winners, not anonymous Internet chat room characters pushing the typical news of the day. Carefully explore the chapters to come. I promise you will be surprised and intrigued at the lessons within.

# Chapter One

# Stick to Your Knitting

*Gary Davis, Jack Forrest,
and Rick Slaughter*

WHILE TODAY SUNRISE CAPITAL IS A VERY SUCCESSFUL money management firm, it did not start that way. It began with three visionary men who dared to be different. They saw opportunity and chased it. One of the founders put it this way: They stick to their knitting. They follow their trading rules. I said this in the Introduction, but it bears repeating: To learn trend following trading, to make a great deal of money with this strategy, requires confidence. The best way to instill that confidence in you is to show you, start to finish, successful traders' paths. As you read this book you may find yourself asking why it is relevant when these traders started. You may be asking why it is relevant to learn about their performance in the 1970s, 1980s, 1990s, and so on. It's relevant because it shows consistency of strategy. This is not some "got lucky trading" method that works for one month, one year, or one decade. It has worked literally month by month for decades. In fact, by the time you finish this book I hope you look carefully at consistency of performance at all times for all strategies—not just trend following. If you find a strategy that doesn't have performance proof behind it, you're gambling. With that out of the way, let's jump in.

If you learn anything from this book, let it be the simple lesson: Stick with it. There will always be distractions: Breaking news banners, surprises, and unpredictable chaotic events are everywhere, but you can't let yourself be fazed. Here is one big secret: Top traders don't pay attention to that stuff. They have found, through hard work, diligent study, and perhaps a little luck— that their ability to stick with a trading plan is far more important than knowing or worrying about what their neighbor is doing.

Go back with me to the mid-1970s. Jack Forrest, a doctor practicing and teaching in San Diego, had built up his savings to begin trading his own account. It wasn't a lot of money, but it was enough to get going. He began investing in stocks, but it didn't take long for him to see that commodity futures, and their big up and down moves, would be much more lucrative.

Like many, Forrest got his start trading with fundamentals—understanding balance sheets, supply, demand, and so on. He realized that his ability to analyze markets was not very good. He talked to local brokers and they had no clue either. No one seemed to have a logical or systematic approach—a *trading system*. Many were just gamblers. Others chalked up their trading to having a feeling for what was going to happen. We have all had those experiences. That's how most everyone is initially exposed to the markets.

----------------------------- ∾ -----------------------------

**Some people say, "Boy, it really looks like fundamental analysis has a lot of potential." If you ask why it has potential, the usual response is "It just does."**

But when you realize that a seat of the pants approach to the markets, otherwise known as using fundamentals, doesn't work, what can you do? Head toward systematic techniques to trade the markets.

That means looking at what has happened historically. It starts with reading stories about famed investors such as Jesse Livermore, Dickson Watts, and Richard Donchian, and other great traders who have used systematic approaches throughout the years. There is no shortage of these kinds of books to check out. One major commonality from these authors and their decades ago wisdom: Get on the big move and stay with it.

The obvious questions: "Well how do you get on the big move?" "Try different things?" "What are those things?" "Buy a set of trading rules from someone else?"

Forrest started experimenting with technical trend trading ideas, and the idea of channel breakouts.

*Channel breakouts* occur when a stock or commodity is trading in a tight channel, then starts trading at a price higher than the top of the channel. What do I mean by tight channel? Apple is trading at 300, 305, 300, 305, 300 and then boom jumps to 325. It is breaking out of the "channel" of tight prices.

As Forrest went along experimenting, buying breakouts was working well, so Forrest began trading that way. Some traders take years to find a profitable system, but

Forrest had some luck on his side in that he found the right kind of approach—an approach very different from what most others were practicing.

With these kinds of trading rules you can become totally systematic. You can write your rules out and follow them with rigid discipline. Forrest's first system was very simple: buying weekly breakouts. It was a 12-week breakout system. Enter long or enter short when the market makes a 12-week high or low.

What markets can you trade like this? While the markets were different when Forrest started—all physical commodities—systematic trend following rules allow you to trade almost all markets today. That means stocks, currencies, gold, oil—you name it.

## Night Class

While Forrest was doing his own research and trading, he had an interesting experience early on. He took a night class from legendary trader Ed Seykota, during the early 1980s. Seykota reinforced trend trading rules and trading psychology.

Seykota was teaching a four-week channel breakout system with a filter—only to be applied if the market was going up (from the long side). He did not apply the system if the market was decreasing (no short selling).

A filter is set up as a hurdle for taking a trade signal (your breakout). You would only trade from the long side if the most recent six-month breakout was up.

---

**Trend following can be simple, but sticking with it is the hard part.**

---

It was more than just rules though. Because Seykota had been so successful with a systematic approach, it gave Forrest the confidence that he too had a shot at that type of success.

It's the same reason I want to introduce you to successful trend following traders throughout this book: to give you that same confidence.

## Teaching Friends

Jack Forrest and Gary Davis were both doctors working in research at the University of California—San Diego. They were also tennis partners. Forrest desperately wanted someone to bounce trading ideas off of and who could trade his same systematic trend trading way, but he had no luck initially finding a trading comrade.

Forrest had about a five-year start on Davis before they even began discussing trading. Even though they were good friends, Davis had no idea of Forrest's trading passion.

How did Davis finally learn of Forrest's passion? It all started with the mention of pork bellies while sitting on the beach after a tennis match. Yes, they were talking pork belly futures contracts—the type traded at the CME. Pork bellies? Just a fancy name for bacon.

While talking about pork bellies on the beach that day, Forrest said that he had "all of these books on trading" and told Davis that if he was interested in learning about the markets he was welcome to borrow them. Davis powered through almost 20 books in a week's time. It was the beginning of his trend following trading career.

Does this sound like an accident? Does this sound like Davis had no preset plan to be a trader? You would be correct. Davis enjoyed his faculty work, but never thought it was the perfect spot for him. He felt like a misfit among the rest of the faculty.

## The First 17 Trades—Losers—or Don't Ask Around

Davis was just about to turn 34 as he started trading with a trend following program he had learned from author J. Welles Wilder, Jr. He lost on his first 17 trades, but once he made one tweak, which he believed is the only reason he is still trading now, he was back in the game.

What was Davis's Aha! moment? Dissect people who have been successful in almost any form of trading long-term and who have been trading some form of trend following or momentum trading.

---

**Successful fundamental traders often have great success because they've been in the right place at the right time.**

---

After recovering from his first big losing streak, Davis realized that he had no idea what anybody else was doing—beyond his book reading. One thing he did know was that most traders last six months and lose all their money. Worse yet, it seemed successful traders lasted three years and then lost all of their money. He expected that his trading career would follow in a similar fashion.

More apt to be involved in independent study, Davis never did like talking to other traders much. He felt the key to his trend trading strategy was to stick with his plan, not changing rules around after looking at someone else and saying, "He has got this great idea. Oh, I'll try that."

As Forrest and Davis were each going down their separate, and growing trading paths, their future partner, Rick Slaughter, had already known for some time that the markets were where he wanted to be. He could remember literally being at his grandfather's knee learning about stocks.

As a young man, corporate law was Slaughters' interest, but plans shifted. On his twenty-first birthday he placed his first trade. He was one of the first to program a trading system into a computer in the 1970s. Not long after, Slaughter set up shop and was trading trend following systems for clients.

## Friends and Family Plan

Davis came to the conclusion, after a period of rigorous and profitable testing with his own money, that there was significant potential in scaling the size of his trading strategies. He sought the help of friends and family for capital to seed a larger pool of money.

Davis founded and launched what would come to be known as Sunrise Capital Partners (known as Sunrise Commodities at the time of inception) in 1980—with the gentle prodding of Ken Tropin (who then was with Dean Witter brokerage, but who today runs one of the most successful trend following firms in the world).

Davis was not super high tech at the time. He preferred handwritten charts and price quotes from the print version of the *Wall Street Journal*. That should be an inspiration for those of you who want to make excuses for not having the perfect this or that. Just do it, right?

However, there is an even larger lesson at play here. Today, many are at a disadvantage in testing their trading ideas. It is a computer-generated love affair now with commercials promoting 24/7. However, it takes experience to be able to recognize what's real and what's luck coming out of the data. Back in the days before the popularization of computers, testing was done by hand. You saw every trade on paper. Everything was obvious. Back then all you needed was to look at a chart, and the longer you looked at a chart, the more you realized how similar they were.

---

**The latest gizmo or hype is not the key to your trading success.**

---

Davis continued on his trajectory of success with Sunrise, and by the mid-1990s was successfully managing over $200 million and routinely delivering double-digit annual returns for investors. Forrest at this point had met and become partners with Rick Slaughter. The two were enjoying success as a team, albeit at a more modest level of assets under management than Davis. Acting on instinct in early 1995, the three industry pioneers merged to form Sunrise Capital Partners.

## Markets Are Not Efficient

Many people think you can't beat the market. Markets are efficient they say. The academics believe it as religion. The story goes something like this: Even if you see a discrepancy in the markets, by the time you try to take advantage of it, it will be gone. So, instead buy a mutual fund and hold on until you are six feet under. Trend followers don't accept that jaded worldview.

Rick Slaughter may have been young, and a touch arrogant about some things in life and perhaps in the markets, but he never bought the *efficient market hypothesis*. When he was exposed to Eugene Fama, the founder of the efficient market hypothesis, he was in graduate school and the theory was just taking hold. Slaughter perceived a hole in it. He could not see how markets were efficient, when he and many of his peers were consistently making money. His thinking, then and now, is vastly different from that of almost all typical Wall Street views.

The reality? Markets are often in "tail" situations that can produce sizable profits—profits that, over time, will significantly outweigh losses that may occur when markets are not operating within tails. When I say *tail*, think back to that stats class you probably hated. The tail of the bell curve is what I mean: extreme events that are supposed to be very rare, but actually happen quite regularly in the markets.

Meaning, we all know the world is chaotic. We know surprises happen. We know that trying to explain the world with a perfectly symmetrical bell curve, a normal distribution, is not smart . . . so why not build a trading strategy to take advantage of that?

How do you do this? Once a potential trend signal is hit within a market, various filtering techniques take place (not exactly the early ones mentioned with Seykota, but in the same spirit). You need to look at the volatility of the market in question and determine whether the movement is simply noise or, instead, the onset of a price trend. Because it is impossible to know the difference in many instances, as a general rule, you should scale back the size of your initial trade in a situation where there is high volatility, placing relatively larger initial trades in times of lower volatility.

The key is to make sure you never miss a potential big trend. You always want to put some kind of trade on when your system says enter as your price trigger hits. If you are wrong, you have stops to protect your capital, to protect your downside.

***

**Believe in the basics: The trend is your friend. It is a powerful tool and that means you can never miss a trade. After all, you never know which move is going to be the mother of all moves.**

One of the lessons you can learn from the men at Sunrise: They jump on every trade; however, how much they risk on those trades changes over time, as well as how many pieces those trades are broken into.

Are most trades going to be profitable? No. But you don't know which ones are going to be winners or losers, so you have to move on every trade. Am I being redundant? Just a little! But this is so important to accept.

Just as you move on every trade, you must protect yourself on every trade. Protecting your downside is critical to trend following success, but sorely taken for granted by most investors—even by the so-called legendary fundamental investors who pollute TV regularly.

## Follow the Leader

Logical rules are mission critical! So do like the leaders do. At the time a trade is placed, regardless of its size, assign it a pre-set stop loss so that in the event a perceived trend immediately reverses, only a very small amount of capital is lost. In addition to this predetermined money stop, all trades should be assigned a pre-set trailing stop that will activate, and then accelerate if a perceived price trend begins to fulfill itself. You do this so if a trend reverses after a

*(Continued)*

run-up in price, at least some of the profits earned from the trade are realized. You want to try to have the highest exposures on when a trend is most likely to continue and the lowest exposures on when a trend is least likely to continue. Generally speaking, you want to trade all markets in a similar fashion. However, there are some markets and sector-specific rules that help differentiate them. It is not unusual to have money stops, trailing stops, and profit targets in a market such as wheat that are different from those used in the euro.

## Expanding Your Horizons

A core theory of trend following is that when markets have a certain movement or momentum, and once they start in motion—they tend to stay in motion.

Have there been changes in the last 30 years to affect these basic beliefs? Sure. Market volatility over the last 30 years has been tremendous, but the change in opportunity has equally been tremendous. Today you have the opportunity to diversify into areas that wouldn't have been possible 30 years ago.

Now, diversification is great, but only if you have the rules set in place to control your moves. Most people just don't do what they're *supposed* to do. Jack Forrest was blunt: "Your trading needs to boil down to rules, money management, and that is it. These are the logical rules, and we don't change them unless we have a good reason to."

Forrest sees your trend following success in simple terms: You can buy rules from someone, make them up yourself, or buy some and make changes so they become your own. But most people aren't willing to put the time in. You should be smiling at that. That's motivating. If most people won't put in the time, or can't do it, or just have some excuse— that opens the door wide for you.

---

**Trend trading is a rollercoaster. Having the wherewithal to stay with it when the rollercoaster is roaring downhill is essential.**

---

It's too easy to find other ways that seem to work at the moment of chaos, but if you're changing your rules around all of the time, you have no chance. Take that to the bank.

## Knowing What You Don't Know

Gary Davis never felt like he knew anything in the beginning. He was an intelligent doctor and worked hard, but approaching trading like a research scientist may have been his real genius. The one thing he firmly understood after trend trading research was that if he didn't follow his plan, he had nothing. It was pretty clear that if he just did it, he'd make money.

One of the nice things about being a *mechanical trader* is that mechanical trading is not time intensive. The research can be time intensive, but the actual trading isn't. You just have rules, you follow them, and you don't deviate.

Almost anybody that follows markets knows that they react in certain ways once momentum starts, and especially as it builds. Moves eventually get excessive, stop, and go the other way. To not understand that about markets is to not understand anything about human nature. Davis saw this early.

## White Noise

Watching the news, reading financial magazines, and listening to the President, is not how you make money in the markets. Davis is clear on this: "You don't make money by explaining how things happen and you don't make money by guessing what's going to happen in the future. You don't know what's going to happen in the future. The things that occur in the future that make you money are all things you couldn't figure out were going to happen."

It always makes for an interesting story to say, "Well, this is going to happen because this or that." That is information everybody already knows. It's already baked into the market price.

Most traders, and most people, think a good result or big profit happens only because they are smart. That is pure fundamental reasoning. Playing your results is a dangerous game. By playing your results, you play into believing your own hype: "If I made money on it, it was a good idea. If I didn't make money on it, it was a bad idea!"

This is not necessarily true. A lot of great trades that should have won don't end up winning, but just because it was a losing trade doesn't make it a bad idea, or make it a wrong trade.

Davis painted the lesson with sports, "You are a football coach. It's fourth and inches and you've got an 85 percent chance of making a first down to end the game, or you can punt, give it to the other team, and you've got a 70 percent chance of winning the game. People will evaluate you on whether you made the first down, not whether you assessed the odds correctly. And if you don't make the first down, many will say it was an awful decision. If you make it, they'll say, 'You had guts.'"

That's the wrong way to think. You want to try and make assessments of the odds. "If I do it this way, what are the odds?" Are the odds with me or are the odds against me? That's something that you can't do very well with fundamental trading.

## The Big Money

I know that you want to get rich in a nice straight line that only goes up. No can do. It doesn't work that way. You can't imagine your account having some volatility? Don't trade! If you're going to trade for yourself and you want the chance to make the big money, you will face periods where your account value can drop significantly. Meaning, if you want the chance for your account to go from 100 to 200, it might go to 60 before it goes to 200. That's life. Does it have to be that volatile? No. In fact, when Sunrise trades for their clients they aim for less return and less *drawdown*. Drawdown is the measurement in both time and money of an account's losing period. These are choices.

The experts who write books on fundamental analysis, appear on financial TV with daily predictions, or worse the ones who write articles saying that you can't be the next Gary Davis, Jack Forrest, or Rick Slaughter—while ignoring 30 years of positive performance—are just wrong. I would argue that critics in the face of performance proof are delusional. Their fears and concerns are a broken record, while at the same time the trend men keep producing.

However, some academics are concluding that taking a systematic approach to the markets is viable. They are learning, as trend traders already know, these strategies can make you money and reduce your overall portfolio risk. You really can take any reasonable systematic approach, track multiple markets, and have the chance to make serious money in the long run.

But don't be fooled—it takes hard work.

People always want the big moneymaking strategies, and they exist, but it takes practice to win—just like learning to play the piano. Most people are not willing to sit down, get a good teacher, and practice. Trend trading success is very analogous to learning an instrument. There's no difference. People would like to make the big money, but no one is going to give it to you. You have to work and do something for it.

That something, in the case of Sunrise Capital, is sticking to an ideology. This is how Sunrise has been able to stay strong as a systematic trend following company. Their success is an inspiration for everyone.

Chapter Two

# Someone's Gotta Lose for You to Win

### *David Druz*

— ❧ —

DAVID DRUZ HAS BEEN TRADING AS A TREND FOLLOWING trader for more than three decades. He, like many in this book, did not start with millions, and when he and I talked he made sure that I understood one of his biggest insights, perhaps the single biggest reason he made his fortune: Life is not fair, and everyone doesn't win. In fact, markets are typically structured with a winner and loser. Druz believes the evidence shows overwhelmingly that somebody has to lose for you to win. That might sound hardcore, but hold your judgment. There is more.

Imagine you have a friend named Charlie, a fraternity brother a couple years ahead of you in college. You are attending the University of Illinois at Urbana-Champaign in the 1970s. Your buddy Charlie starts trading with $2,000 and a year later has run that up to around $500,000. Oh sure, Charlie appears to be brilliant in his trading and absolutely fearless, but how is he doing it?

After graduation Charlie comes back to school on weekends to visit his girlfriend. He always has wads of bills in his pockets. Many guys in the frat love it because Charlie buys rounds and rounds at the college bars. But wasn't there at least one guy who wanted to know how Charlie did it, instead of how much he could spend on bad keg beer?

David Druz was that one guy. He pestered Charlie and ultimately landed his first job through him. Druz ended up working at the Chicago Board of Trade (now the CME Group) during summer vacations. This was tedious work in the research department of a brokerage house. Lots of paperwork and not exactly real close to the moneymaking action on the floor.

---

**You have to want success. You can't be halfway there. Go all in. Go for it!**

Druz took computer programming in college and had been given leeway at the brokerage firm to play around with his programming ideas. He had a knack for testing trading ideas—meaning, "What happens if you always buy here and sell there?" He soon started working on his first trend following mockups (what he would call *systems*) during those summer breaks.

He was in his own world, happy to not know anything about anything. Do you ever feel that way? All he knew was colloquial stock market wisdom that had been circulating among all Chicago traders. At the time the buzz was all about "the big cycle." People were talking about four-week cycles and six-month cycles and so on. Amazingly, there are people today nearly 40 years later promoting the exact same drivel on CNBC and across Internet chat rooms.

Druz soon determined there were no cycles and that daily news guys and prediction prognosticators were full of baloney. Although he had figured out that there were no persistent cycles, Druz still didn't assume anything going forward. He would hear people declare this or that, and he would respond, "I'm going to test that. I'm going to see if it's true." That's how he got his feet wet testing trading systems.

Once again, testing a trading system means having a rule to buy here and a rule to sell there. Once you have established a rule, you take market prices; Apple, silver, oil, or gold (who cares, the market!), and you test it to see if your buy and sell rules work for making money.

Even though he loved his job in the markets, Druz soon entered medical school to hedge his bets. Yet he still took his vacations at the brokerage firm—working. Medicine was interesting to him, but he was 100 percent fascinated with the markets.

Did he have lots of money? No. The only money he had was $5,000 in stock that his father had given him. Druz cashed that out and put it into his account. At that same time the brokerage firm offered him a job, a full-time job to quit medical school and go work for them. They offered Druz $50,000 to start. That was really good money in the 1970s.

A slightly drunk friend told him, "Dave, don't take that job. You can be a really good trader, but if you take that job, you'll never be a great trader. You've got to get a nest egg for security. You don't want to trade with scared money. Finish medical school, be a doctor, and then you'll be a great trader."

Does that make sense to you? Maybe not at first blush, but it was the wisest piece of information anyone ever told Druz. He has since seen many people over the years trading with scared money—meaning they would make decisions on the value of the money to them (read: emotional decisions about a new car, suit, or wife), and not follow the exact rules of their trading plan. "Don't quit your day job" is another critical success lesson—write it down and tape it over your desk.

Druz took his $5,000 and started to trade. He wasn't very good at first, and his account dropped down to around $1,500. At that point he had hit rock bottom and trading success was beginning to move out of sight.

He then received a message from his brokerage firm, "You got a fill on your trade." Druz said, "I don't have any orders in. I'm out of business." The brokerage replied, "No, you had a 'Good Til Cancelled' order (GTC) in and it is 'limit up'." Druz was back in business! The universe apparently would not allow him to quit—he truly believed that.

You too might think sometimes, "If I only had one more chance," but when the next opportunity or chance does come around again you have to be willing to get in the game and play again—without thinking about your negative first experience. Second chances are telling you something. Heed their advice.

## The Chart Doctor Finds A Mentor

After trading on his own for some time, Druz was doing well enough that other doctors around took notice. His first trend following fund began in 1981 purely because other doctors at the hospital wanted their money traded.

Doctor Druz, however, was getting burned out from a hectic emergency room schedule—no normal sleep! He was faced with a choice. The markets were his passion, and he could see himself going that direction for the long run. So in 1991, about nine years into private practice, burnout officially hit.

Although he was doing very well without formal training, Druz wanted a mentor. He had read *Market Wizards* and Ed Seykota was the star. It just so happened that Seykota was famous for teaching many top trend followers going back to the 1970s.

*Market Wizards* alluded to the fact that Seykota lived near Lake Tahoe and so, as luck would have it, Druz happened to be near Lake Tahoe one day and stopped at 7-Eleven to look in their phone book. Seykota was listed. Druz wrote his number down, and got back on a plane headed for home.

When he got the courage to call him, Seykota answered. They talked for a little bit about trading and Seykota said, "Why don't you send me some of your trades and call me in a week and we'll talk again?"

Druz got off the phone and began copying charts. He drew in the trades where he entered, where he exited, and where his initial stops were. He sent them express mail to Seykota.

The next week Druz called Seykota. He didn't recall their conversation. Seykota said, "I talk to a lot of guys.

I talk to guys all the time." Druz said, "You told me to send you all of my trades and to call you!"

Druz was frustrated, "Ed, look around your desk. Do you have an express mail envelope there?" "Yeah, I got one." "Did you open it?" "No, I haven't opened it." "Well, open it." Druz was upset that he had stayed up two nights in a row preparing all the charts. Seykota finally began looking through the charts and said, "Oh. This is really interesting. I see what you're doing here. You trade a lot like I do. But there are a few things you need to work out. Why don't you come be my apprentice?"

You can't help but think of the classic *Star Wars* scenes with Yoda counseling Luke Skywalker: "Do or do not . . . there is no try."

Druz became Seykota's first official in-house apprentice.

It was the most remarkable experience of his life. It was Zen. Druz saw Seykota as a genius. Not just smart, but like Einstein or Mozart. Given that I had spent time with Seykota too, I knew what Druz was talking about.

Seykota sees through you. You have no defense mechanisms. Most of us go through life with mechanisms to protect ourselves, but with Seykota, forget it. You're totally bare-naked, so to speak, and it's hard on the psyche. It was initially very hard for Druz to deal with.

However, the experience with Seykota gave Druz confidence. Do you ever do that? Reach out for help? Reach out for a mentor even when you are already having great success?

There is always more to learn. New insights, especially psychological ones captured through another person, are the hallmark of a true winning trend following ethos.

## The Source of Profits

Long trend following track records are not luck. If they were pure happenstance then Druz, for example, wouldn't trade for clients.

He believes the reason trend following traders have an edge goes back to a common sense realization tracing back to his early training at the brokerage firm. Trend traders are trying to capture risk premium from the hedgers. What does that mean?

*Hedgers* are a type of market player. They typically have a position in one market in an attempt to offset exposure in some opposite position. The hope is to minimize their exposure to unwanted risk. *Speculators* (i.e., trend followers) assume risk for hedgers. Speculators accept risk in the futures markets, aiming to profit from the very price change that hedgers are protecting themselves against.

Hedgers who trade futures are in the risk transfer business. They receive insurance against adverse price moves. What are *futures*? A contractual agreement, generally made on the trading floor of a futures exchange, to buy or sell a particular commodity or financial instrument at a predetermined price in the future. Futures contracts detail the quality and quantity of the underlying asset; they are standardized to facilitate trading on a futures exchange. The U.S. federal regulatory agency of the futures industry is called the Commodity Futures Trading Commission (CFTC). Whereas some futures contracts may call for physical delivery of the asset, others are settled in cash. The terms "futures contract" and "futures" refer to essentially the same thing.

Hedgers are net losers in futures markets over the long run, and Druz's trend trading approach is based on capturing this risk premium.

The idea is that you want to buy strength (buy high, not low) and sell weakness (sell short as the price drops), which is the opposite of hedging behavior. Your winning trades as a trend following trader will be less frequent, but larger on average. These winning trades happen when prices strengthen or weaken well beyond expectations— which is when big trends form.

You can tell when the hedgers, as a group, go from long to short and short to long. They are always on the wrong side of the big moves—primarily because, unlike speculators, they are using the markets to protect themselves. Druz thought, "This makes total sense," and realized his real trading opportunity was to capitalize on their losses. The job of the hedgers is to transfer risk and lock in business profits for their company. Their job is not to make money in the futures markets. Their job is to utilize those markets to allow them to run an efficient business.

You can never lose sight of the fact that the futures markets are a zero sum game (for every winner there is a loser). For you to win, someone has to lose. It's astonishing that many never consider this.

However, if your trading plan stays opposite hedgers, if you employ good money management (meaning you don't bet the farm on every trade), and you diversify (trade more than one market), you can find a mathematical edge to win in the long run. Stay consistent over time with that strategy, and you can make the big money.

By being opposite hedgers, Druz became a trend follower by default, not by design. This is in contrast to trading systems that are specifically designed to capture trends (which is the successful approach seen in most other chapters of this book).

## Keep It Simple and Start Small

Do you need a really big company to be a trend follower? Do you need a company at all? It's unfortunate that many think you need a large research staff of hundreds of PhDs, or a large firm established in a finance capital like London or New York to be successful. That is definitely not the case. Druz is proof positive that you do not need a large overhead to produce large profits.

Look at Ed Seykota, for example. Druz noted that Seykota doesn't have a staff and he blows most of his competition out of the water. It's just him.

If you are working with very short term trading, or sophisticated PhD stuff (whatever that might be), that's a whole different game. Maybe you do need a PhD army for different trading strategies, but we are not discussing those strategies here.

---

### Follow the Leader

Designing your own trading system can seem complicated at first. If you design a system to capitalize on longer-term trends, once you appropriately integrate portfolio-selection and money management strategies (extremely important!), it is surprising that your choice of system or parameters thereof is often quite uncritical over the long run. Certain types of systems do perform better than others, and selecting

(*Continued*)

certain clusters of variables within a system will affect system performance.

But what really counts is this: Once a system's algorithms and parameters are established, the system must be followed exactly and religiously. A system cannot be second-guessed or used intermittently. Values of variables cannot be altered. Parameters cannot be arbitrarily changed. A robust system works over many types of market conditions and over many timeframes. It works in German Bund futures and it works in wheat. It works when tested over 1950–1960 or over 1990–2000. Robust systems tend to be designed around successful trading tactics not designed around specific types of markets or market action. And here is the amazing thing about robust systems: The more robust a system, the more volatile it tends to be!

Druz gives this advice: "There are whole families of trend trading ideas that seem to work forever on any market. The down side is they are very volatile because they are never curve-fit. They're never exactly fit to any particular market or market condition. But over the long run, they do extract money from the market. You want to be focused on how you divvied up the risk in your portfolio, how much risk you take in each market, how many contracts you trade in each market, that's the stuff that really counts . . . if you have money management wired, you can let volatility go because you know it doesn't have any correlation with the risk of ruin. You can use volatility to your advantage."

## "Put your Affection on Portfolio Selection!"

Trend following is not rocket science. You can do this, but you are going to want to focus on one area more than you might imagine. Often neglected, but an extraordinarily important ingredient in your trend following trading, is your portfolio selection and portfolio weighting. Let's take a look at some recent markets. By far one of the most amazing markets of the last few years has been cotton.

Now, let's suppose you had a portfolio that consisted of one market and you happen to pick cotton. Any kind of trend trading system you use would make money. Now, let's suppose that you pick cocoa. Almost any kind of trend system that you come up with would not make money. Success was completely dependent on which market you picked.

Many times, over the years, systems traders have contacted Druz for his help. They'll send him their track records and say, "Here is my system, can you give me any advice?" He invariably will look at what markets they are trading and can tell right away whether or not portfolio selection was considered.

Many miss the importance of portfolio selection completely. You can make rules to narrow down your portfolio to something manageable from the thousands of markets available.

What is a key lesson about portfolio selection? There's a pervasive mindset that every market should be weighted equally. That's not true. It doesn't work that way. Druz learned that from Seykota.

Seykota had a trade on in the German Bund. Seykota decided to add more to his Bund position. Druz said, "Ed, you already have a Bund trade on." Seykota looked at Druz like he was from the moon and said, "Oh." Druz continued, "Now you can diversify. You don't want to be correlated?" Seykota plainly, but with great wit and wisdom, said, "The Bund is the best market out there now."

Druz said, "I think we should really take a trade in T-bonds for diversification." Seykota did not see the logic. He saw Bunds as the best market at the time and explained that he was going to continue taking another trade in Bunds instead of T-bonds.

This is not saying that you want to put all your eggs in one basket, that's not the concept, but the idea is that your weightings of the markets don't need to be uniform. That simple Seykota wisdom hit Druz. It was an Aha! moment.

## Stick Around for the Dance

In a world where people fixate on buying low or cheap, don't forget that some trend following traders don't get into markets until they are so scarily high that you might feel it is crazy to still buy. That mentality runs square against almost every common Wall Street axiom over the last hundred years, but it is exactly how Druz has made a quiet fortune while staring out over the Pacific from his Hawaii home.

And you don't have to have a thousand PhDs in your organization to trade trend-trading rules. Don't give up, and don't think just because you don't have the so-called right background or degree, or that you don't have a huge staff, that you can't be a trader making big money.

The Druz experience is all about getting the little guy to see himself making money. The little guy can win. Druz is proof.

---

**Your goal is to be around forever making money at this game. The best way you can go about that is by making it hard to be knocked out.**

---

Chapter Three

# No Guts, No Glory

*Paul Mulvaney*

PAUL MULVANEY WANTS TO MAKE THE MOST MONEY possible over the course of his lifetime. And so far he's headed in the right direction. Mulvaney is known as the trend following trader who made over 100 percent in 2008, but I'm willing to bet that there will be more 100 percent years to come. His insights are especially useful for readers who still dream about getting rich—not the opportunity for a couple of thousand dollars a month in retirement income living at Del Boca Vista Phase III (*Seinfeld* fans are with me).

Look at baseball. The home run hitter is the one we pay to see. Everyone wants to be there when a 500-foot home run is blasted into the upper deck. Even if you know nothing about baseball, balls hit far into blue sky inspire awe.

Trading is no different. Making the most money possible is what captures our imagination. It's what we all want, even if some of us are deathly afraid to admit it. Unfortunately, in today's culture, wealth building is something frowned on, especially if you end up with more than your neighbor.

That attitude did not stop Paul Mulvaney. He generated returns of 11.6 percent and 45.5 percent in September and October 2008, at the exact time Lehman Brothers' collapse was scaring the wits out of everyone. Home runs? An understatement. Unapologetic wealth creation—check.

Is he a trend follower? Yes.

Mulvaney's returns challenge the widespread view that trading based on mathematical models, the ones built on historical chart patterns and trends, don't work. His full-year return in 2008 was in excess of 100 percent. That return should grab you by the throat with some discomfort. Where did those returns come from?

## Numbers Obsession

Mulvaney started programming computers in his mid-teens during the late 1970s. Programming at an early age instilled a systematic mindset that carried into college and into business. Initially he did in-depth trend trading research while working at Merrill Lynch. And by the time he had left to hang up his own shingle, he had devised essentially the trend trading system he uses today.

The start, his launch, was in essence, "Other trend following traders have been very successful. I can be too." From there he proved their success and techniques to himself. He dug deeper, learning and testing his ideas against their achievements so he too could be very successful.

Mulvaney tried to find out everything he could about everyone else's profitable trend trading, but it only amounted to snippets. There was not a lot of trend trading detail in his world at the time.

His background allowed him to begin writing trading simulations (think TradeStation® today). It was second nature to him. Programming was what he was trained to do.

It was not that difficult to come up with a simple trend following model and test it. Knowing that there were big trend following firms profitable over long periods of time, and that they were all using similar trend following strategies, his direction was set.

Discovering channel breakouts has been a link throughout numerous start-up stories. Mulvaney was no different. He exits positions at a predetermined stop-loss point. Nothing emotional, like breaking news, ever leads him to override his system, not even a shock event (think the Japan earthquake).

His entry methods have always been simple (read: breakouts). It's what happens later that matters. Preparing for what could happen is what you should be spending most of your time on. How you compute the amount you are willing to risk for every trade, and how you exit your big winners, that's what counts.

I quickly learned other key, big picture principles and lessons from Mulvaney.* These points are not about a particular linear order. These are crucial pieces of the puzzle that just need to be absorbed:

- Don't be afraid to trade smaller and more obscure markets. Orange juice? Trade it. It works. You can make money there.

- Strive to produce a home run out of every trend that you can get money on. But every trade has a defined stop-loss point, so you know exactly how much you can lose. If the trade starts to go in your direction you only exit if it starts to turn against you. Make no predictions about how far a trend

---

*See: "Trend Following and the MCM System—An Interview with Paul Mulvaney." The full interview is available at www.trendfollowing.com/whitepaper/mulvaney.pdf.

might run. You just let it go because you can never know how far it might go. All you know is that when a market starts to move, there are forces that you can't understand at work. Don't ask, "Why?"

- Aim to make high absolute returns in rising or falling markets. You want to generate returns in all market conditions by taking long or short positions across a diversified range of markets.

- Markets don't move from one state to another in a straight line; there are periods of shock and volatility. You have to deal with those unsettling but inevitable events, but there are many, many commercial systems that have been generating strong, albeit volatile, returns for a long time. Mulvaney opined: "There are definitely firm grounds for believing in Santa Claus."*

- You want your trend following method to be very general. You want it to continue to work, meaning it can't be dependent on any unique set of market characteristics. Trend following's robustness and volatility go hand-in-hand. The ability to take punches to the chin and remain robust is part of the reason you will be able to thrive and survive.

---

*Michael Covel, *Trend Following: Learn to Make Millions in Up or Down Markets* (Upper Saddle River, NJ: Person Education Inc., 2009), 17.

- Unfortunately, despite all of the evidence, many find it hard to accept the inherent return in trend following. They like to argue that trend following is lucky. You should pursue trend following because of its superior absolute profitability. If friends, brokers, or your professors don't get it—that's fine. They don't know and you can't expect them to know unless they are doing the same homework as you.

- Go try trading using fundamentals alone. Go lose some serious money. Isn't amassing a comprehensive set of economic data for all markets worldwide impossible? It is vital to focus on what is happening rather than on what should happen. Trend following is about what is happening now. It is a very pragmatic strategy. Never lose sight of the famous saying by John Maynard Keynes: "Markets can remain irrational longer than you can remain solvent."

- There is no perfect trading system. It's like being able to define the perfect game of golf or tennis. You can only compare one person's game against another's. There is no absolute answer. Some trade for huge returns, some trade for moderate returns. It is a choice you need to make.

- Should you trade short-term trends? Unequivocally, trend followers should go for the long term—trends

that can extend for over a year. Long-term trading avoids the short-term randomness inherent in
markets.

- Don't take profits. What do I mean? If the market
  is up, don't get out because you think you already
  have *enough* profit. Exit on your stop losses only.
  Profit taking interferes with the unlimited upside
  potential that you want to have, in theory, on every
  trade.

- If you have a system, and you regularly override
  your system, you are essentially waving goodbye to
  the incredibly valuable body of statistical research
  from all trend followers over the last 30 years.

- As a trader, you always want to prevent drawdowns
  from occurring, but trying to avoid them completely
  is absurd. In fact, it's not volatile trading that you
  should be scared of; rather it's trading that promises to make you money every month. That's the
  strategy where you wake up one day broke.

- Sticking to your system is much more important
  than the actual details of the system. It's you against
  the world, not you and your buddies commiserating
  in a chat forum.

- Mulvaney's trend trading is profitable on 54 to
  55 percent of days, but on only 25 percent of trades.
  Obviously those 25 percent of trades are more

profitable than the 75 percent of trades that are losers. Many traders have a hard time accepting the numbers. If they only dig a little deeper they can see the profit margin.

## No Prediction

If you turn on CNBC you will see talking heads spouting daily about forecasting and prediction. They can't all be full of it? We really can't predict? Econometric researchers have tried to forecast or predict where markets were supposedly headed for decades, but they continually fail. Have they rightfully and finally concluded that it is a fool's errand to try and predict the future? No, I don't think so! They will never stop.

Trend following strategy, taking a completely different philosophical stance, is built on surprises, not predictions. When surprises are planned for in your trading strategy, when predictions are known as folly from the outset, it is much easier to sit back and let the market run its course.

That means, of course, saying no to the efficient market hypothesis (EMH). The markets are clearly inefficient enough that trend followers, using fairly uncomplicated trend following rules, can and have made serious money for decades.

If enough traders have won with trend following over enough time using broadly similar techniques, then that can only mean the markets are inefficient, and wise investors and traders should take advantage of it.

I covered many top trend followers in my first book, *Trend Following*. John W. Henry (owner of the Boston Red Sox), Dunn Capital, Campbell and Company, and Millburn Ridgefield were some of the early trend firms that influenced Mulvaney.

He could look up to them, see their success, and be inspired. Undoubtedly, they all shaped his belief that he too could be a trend trading success.

However, Mulvaney doesn't believe that he is on the cutting edge of trend following technology because there is no cutting edge technology in terms of trend following. He admits to his system's being quite old fashioned. That is how you should view it too. Let's look at a few more of his big picture principles.

- Prices are random variables. That's all they are. Does that mean if someone asked you what markets you were trading you could look at them and say, "You know what, I have no idea, absolutely no idea what market I am trading. It's just a number." Yes, you could say that!
- You don't need to know anything about the fundamentals. You are a *data miner* who looks at data objectively and emotionally to try and find a way to

profit. It's a game, folks. It's the board game Risk. Play the numbers.

- Be prepared to risk a certain percent in each market before your stop is hit. If you have many positions on at the same time, that can lead to high daily, weekly, or monthly swings in your account balance. There is always a non-zero chance that things can blow up and you lose everything, but there has to be risk to obtain that reward.

- Unlike David Druz, Mulvaney sees other speculators as the source of his profits. Looking back at September and October of 2008, much of his gain came from short positions in stock index futures. Who was long in stock index futures? During that time it could only be speculators.

How does it work out in practice as Mulvaney willingly risks it all to achieve his big money returns? Look at his top 10 trades over the years (Exhibit 3.1). Look at how critical it is to not miss a trade. The percent of profit derived from certain big trends can make your whole year.

## Sticking With It

I am not saying trading is easy. After all, how much good in life comes easy? But if you stick with your strategy through thick and thin, and master it, you have a chance

**Exhibit 3.1    Top 10 Trades since Inception**

| Sector | Long/Short | Start | End | Contribution % |
|---|---|---|---|---|
| Interest Rates | Long | Nov 2000 | May 2003 | 66.57 |
| Currencies | Long | Feb 2000 | Nov 2005 | 50.47 |
| Copper | Long | Sep 2003 | May 2006 | 44.64 |
| Petroleum | Long | Jun 1999 | Oct 2000 | 29.18 |
| Grains | Long | May 2007 | Feb 2008 | 28.34 |
| Stocks | Long | May 2005 | Feb 2007 | 26.63 |
| Stocks | Short | Sep 2008 | Mar 2009 | 25.31 |
| Precious Metals | Long | Nov 2005 | Apr 2006 | 23.08 |
| Natural Gas | Long | Mar 2000 | Dec 2000 | 21.05 |
| Stocks | Short | Sep 2000 | Mar 2003 | 16.06 |

*Source:* www.mulvaneycapital.com.

at real freedom—not being stuck with Suze Orman or Dave Ramsey droning on about reducing credit card debt or how to debt finance your house. (By the way, how has that advice worked out for millions? Exactly.)

That said, there are horror stories about people who abandoned their systems at the wrong time. They always say, "If I just would have stuck with it!" Well, they didn't, and in some cases the decision to stray from their long held approach was a career-ending move. Discipline is a critical factor as you head down the trend-trading path.

Let me give an example about sticking with it. The biggest crises Mulvaney had was during July and August 2007, where he had his two biggest down months consecutively. A 42 percent drawdown was the result. In the aftermath he went back and reexamined everything. He examined every possible misstep, considered all assumptions, but in the end concluded that the system was valid.

One of the tests performed in the aftermath was rerunning his trading results against a whole range of different levels of leverage. Mulvaney is notorious for managing his leverage—even if he uses a lot of it.

However, Mulvaney objectively asked what would have happened if he traded with more or less leverage than he actually used? He discovered that had he used lower leverage he would have actually generated a bigger drawdown (read: bigger loss) during the crisis.

That seems intuitive, does it? Hold your judgment.

When his account finally bottomed in August 2007 at the depths of a 42 percent drop, a new gold position kicked in and started making money. By the end of August, he had made new money and had crawled away from the low of his drawdown. At a lower level of leverage, theoretically, he would have captured a smaller recovery from those new gold positions that were kicking in, and actually his system would have taken a slightly larger maximum drawdown.

I just saved you *and* made you a fortune.

Another interesting lesson you can take from 2007? And let me say if you are not understanding why 2007 is related to 2011 and beyond—you are still not with me about trend following.

For that year the best performing single market for Mulvaney was the Canadian dollar. The worst performing market was the Australian dollar. When you put those charts up on the wall, staple them up there, on the face of it they look highly correlated (zigging and zagging at the same time). In fact, those two currencies are reasonably correlated most of the time, but the Australian dollar was too volatile during this time period to make money. From a trend following perspective it kept going down and stopping out, then going back up and forcing a reentry. This kept happening with lots of small losses. It pays to examine facts and not just think you know. Let the numbers win.

---

**Be objective. Subjective analysis is for long-term losers.**

---

## Risk and Volatility

Many equate risk with volatility. They think big returns that come from high reward trend following systems (like Mulvaney's) are much, much riskier than actuality. In fact, acceptance of higher risk in a trend following investment can actually lower the risk of your stock and bond portfolios because when trend following zigs, typical stock and bond investments zag. However, that is a very difficult concept to get people to accept.

Risk of ruin, otherwise known as taking too much risk so you have no more money, has to be your foundation. Mulvaney, for example, will only stop trading his system if his account value drops to a point where he can't trade his strategy. So risk of ruin is that real point where he can't actually trade all of the markets that his system dictates to trade.

Believing in the value of your system to the extent that you would continue trading until you literally didn't have a dollar of capital left to trade is the conviction of a winner. The lesson? If you can avoid blowing up, you should continue to trade your trend following system. That's the only way to get rich. Or, maybe, you can invent the next Facebook. That's another option.

---

### Follow the Leader

Sit in on part of my interview with Mulvaney to hear more of what makes him a leader to follow.

Covel:      When you talk about creating terminal wealth what do you mean exactly? Bill Dunn is approaching 80 years old and he's clearly not dialed it back from the chase for big returns. Trend following legend Richard Donchian traded into his 90s. How do you perceive your trading as you move forward in life? Do you perceive there'll be a time where you change your desire for absolute returns or do you say, "You know what, I'm 46 years old. This is what I love. This is what I want to do and I'm going to try and hit the biggest home run I can over the course of a lifetime"?

Mulvaney:    Yes. Just keep going for the home run. If I take a 100 percent drawdown while trying to make that home run, then fine. Then I'll say, "Well, great, I had a great run at it." I have had two separate 12-month periods when I generated over 100 percent. Eventually when or if I overdid it, and it brought me down, great, I would still not be dissatisfied with my career if that happens.

Covel:    I was speaking to a very successful firm with a 30-year track record. They give the client what he wants, which

*(Continued)*

is less volatility. However, the guys that run it said, "We don't trade for less returns for our personal accounts. In our personal accounts, we want to get rich. We trade for trend following absolute returns."

Mulvaney:   That's what I do. Most good traders take more risk with their own money than they will with client money.

# Chapter Four

# In a Land Far, Far Away from Wall Street

## *Kevin Bruce*

YEARS AGO I INTERVIEWED FOR A TRADING JOB AT SALOMON Brothers in New York City. That was in 1994 and the firm was still very powerful. I still can recall seeing their massive football field–size trading floor at the top of World Trade Center Seven, which was lost on 9/11. At the time, long before I ever knew about trend following, *that* seemed to be the only way you could get rich trading.

Kevin Bruce is living proof that there is no need to be in New York, London, or Chicago—flaunting a sharp business suit and trading in a sky rise. Bruce is a small-town guy from Georgia with no ancestral connection to Wall Street, who has not only made it on Wall Street but conquered it. Heed his path.

Bruce spends his time far away tucked in quiet spots in Richmond, Virginia. He works out six times a week at his local YMCA, and still drives his 1996 Ford pickup. With a net worth of nearly $100 million, he prefers to live life just as he always did before making that fortune. He is low profile. Most people have no idea of his wealth. He says, "I guess that means I've done a pretty good job of just being me."*

He follows a trading strategy first developed while he was a graduate student in finance at the University of Georgia. His strategy tells him when to buy and sell and how much to buy or sell, based on the odds of that trade being a winner or a loser. He trades in all markets across the board. You name the market and he trades it. Does he have expertise in all of these markets? No.

To be a trend following trader, your trading approach must work equally on all markets. You do not want to say,

*Paula C. Squires, "Betting on Futures: Trader Comes Up More Than Even," *Virginia Business*, June 2004.

"I'm going to trade this system in the yen and this system in corn and this system in some other market." If your system is not good enough to work on all markets, then it should not be used.

However, waking up with that principle in your head would probably not occur naturally. Nor did it for Bruce. He went to the University of Georgia in the late 1970s and took a course in agricultural economics. It was mostly oriented towards hedgers (think farmers trying to protect their crop values six months before the harvest season), but in order to keep students interested in the class the teacher had to get creative. He let the students practice trying to make real money by keeping track of hypothetical trades (called paper trading). It was all "I will buy here and sell there" rules.

Bruce's work to develop a mechanical trading system germinated completely from the desire to win the trading game. He ended up beating his classmates in the contest. How did he do? At the beginning of the year he had $10,000, and three months later it was $30,000. Of course, it was only paper money and trading is easy when there is no real money on the line, but the trend following methodology he had developed was sound.

What would you do? What would you take from that experience? From his hypothetical trading experience in college Bruce decided, "Why not try it for real?" He was

22 years old and opened up a small account at his local brokerage—just like many of us have done at one time or the other. No more practice trading! It was real dollars and cents time.

At the end of the year the $5,000 that Bruce had saved from odd jobs had mushroomed into $14,000—all from trend trading. He figured he had made it big. Bruce went and bought a Barcalounger, a 19-inch RCA color TV, and the biggest set of stereo speakers he could find. Why not, right? Splurging on a big win is something we all like to do. However, don't judge that spending binge just yet—freedom was the real goal.

While Bruce was crafty in his early trading, almost tripling his initial seed money, he was really crafty in the way he built up his $5,000 nest egg. When he was about 15, he started the practice of packing a lunch and taking it to school. The cafeteria food wasn't great, but he could buy a lunch for just 35 cents. Bruce would meet other kids in the bathroom daily and auction off his home-style lunch. He would then eat the cafeteria lunch—and would usually net about $2. Nice trade!

In the late 1970s, $5,000 was a pretty good sum of money, but that money was there for him to pay for his college. It was an enormous risk to be trading that money. If he lost the $5,000, that was it.

However, Bruce was so confident in his trading research that he was willing to risk it all without blinking. In fact, there was no doubt that if he lost the $5,000, he would have tried it again, because he had absolute conviction.

---

**The great trend followers do not quit. They practice. They learn. They stick with it.**

---

## Teach Yourself to Be Great

Can you teach yourself to trade? Do you realize how important learning on your own is if you really want to be a successful trader? Everything about Bruce's trading is self-taught. He started in the basement of the University of Georgia library: The school had old editions of the *Wall Street Journal* on microfilm. In the basement dungeon, he would compile his own record of the open, high, low, and closing prices for all markets.

At the time, Bruce was actually working at a gas station at night, and between cleaning bugs off windshields and pumping gas, he had time to think and research—which is where he would analyze that price data. Bruce had a Texas Instruments handheld calculator that helped him sort through price data collected from the library. He figured out how to mathematically define a trend (in order to profit from its movement). It was a basic trend trading system. It was the same system he had used for the trading game in school with slight tweaks. Ultimately, it was the same one he would use with real money in the decades to follow.

## Focus on the Show!

You have no focus? You can't find focus? Stop now. Throw this book away and go do something else.

Seriously.

Look at what Bruce accomplished. He never paid attention to what was going on around him, even after taking an initial bank job after college. While he was working at early bank and brokerage jobs, he would go to lunch with the office guys because that was what was done on typical corporate days. Some of the guys traded cotton, others traded soybeans, but it all depended on what their favorite market was—which did not make much sense to Bruce. Why should you have a favorite market? You should not!

Initially, Bruce wanted to be a corporate lawyer. His uncle, a judge at the time, convinced him that 60-hour work weeks were probably not the lifestyle he wanted. And even if he stuck it out for a law career, the big money wouldn't come until he eventually became a partner. He thought, "I don't like the sound of that."

---

**Figure out early what you want to be.
If you really want to be a trend following
trader—start now!**

---

Bruce had figured out at 22 that he wanted to be a trader. Many of us never figure it out. We never decide. We just go through the motions, hoping for the lottery gods to smile on us.

Even if you decide that you know the way you want to go, there will be obstacles. After graduation Bruce went to work for a fairly sizeable savings bank in Atlanta, but they were risk adverse and would not let him trade his trend following way.

Later he shifted to a small bank in North Carolina and stayed for about four years—since they gave him the opportunity to trade. It was a move up. Finally, in 1986, he landed a bank job in Virginia where he could trade as he wanted—with the opportunity to make big trend trading money.

His motivations were never about a desire to have a Lear jet, a Rolls Royce, or three beach houses, but growing up in a lower middle-class family in a small town in Georgia showed him first-hand how people lived who never aspired for more than what they grew up with. Bruce saw how little freedom that mindset granted, and he wanted no part of it.

Do you want to have a boss telling you what to do? Do you want to be able to go on vacation when you want? Do you ever just want freedom? That was Bruce's motivation.

## Playing Games

I have found, in all of my research into trend following and great trend following traders, that games have played a crucial role. Around the age of 10, Bruce's brother taught him how to play chess. An early lesson was to let your opponent make small mistakes early in the game while looking ahead to take advantage later on.

Bruce once had the opportunity to go to New York and see one of the major brokerage firms' trading floors. He found it like Battle Star Galactica, with more screens and lights than you could imagine. He decided: "I couldn't think in this environment." You can never make decisions when the market is open; everything is like a flight plan, it's got to be pre-planned. Trying to make decisions when the market is open is going to lead to emotional decisions. Everything must be thought out ahead of time. Know what you are going to do if it goes up, if it goes down, and if it doesn't do anything. When all that is figured out, you put your system on autopilot. It almost sounds too simple, but that's the way you need to do it, and that's why you don't need to stress out about anybody's opinion.

If you get a couple of pawns ahead in the game and start trading pieces of equal value—you can lay the groundwork for winning. You trade your bishop for your opponent's bishop, your knight for their knight. When you get down to the end of the game you can end up with two pawns and a king and they've only got the king. In chess, if you can take your pawns and advance them all the way to the other end of the board you can turn them into a queen—which is the most powerful piece on the board.

It is the same in trading. Your opponent's mistakes early in the game can be used to win the game later. How does that exactly translate into trading? It's about finding your edge, your edge to win the game. You need to learn that you need an edge to win. (See Larry Hite's example of edge and expectation in Chapter 5.)

## Risk!

When Bruce initially began his last bank job in 1986, they had a way to measure the risk of their trading with a concept called a risk unit. A risk unit was the equivalent to the market risk on one 30-year Treasury bond. Initially Bruce's allowable risk units were 10. He could take the market risk of 10 Treasury bonds. They may have been equal to two Canadian dollars or five Swiss francs or six corn contracts (remember futures are traded on exchanges like the CME Group; futures trade in contracts and stocks trade in shares).

Soon the bank realized that Bruce's style of trend following trading was minting money and they ramped up Bruce's risk units over time. As his trading progressed, and continued to grow, bank management became more confident in Bruce, and more importantly, he became more confident in his own trading. His trend following trading soon turned very large. It was especially large for a publicly traded, sleepy, midsize southern bank not really expected to be making money as a trend following trader.

There is a larger lesson here for you, though. Risk, and measuring that risk, should always be first in line. However, to the detriment of many, risk and measuring it are often ignored. There is great truth in the idea that if you take care of the downside, the upside will take care of itself. That means you have to have money to play the game. Protect yourself from losing all of your money, and when the big trend comes you can ride it.

One of the big mistakes you can make is to always look up at the stars and think about how much money you are going to earn off a trade. If you do not look down first, trouble! In every situation you need to think about what can go wrong and what will you do if it does go wrong?

Where do you get that discipline? It can begin when you are very young. It can begin with sports or chess or other forms of competition. You start to understand that you can only win if you're consistent. If you do not do the right thing over and over, you don't excel at it. No excellence, no reward.

## Build on a Foundation of Confidence in Your System and in Yourself

All successful trend following traders bring a unique story of how they made it to their understanding, but more importantly they all bring a unique element critical to their success. Bruce's distance from Wall Street may have been his secret weapon. He did not play the Wall Street game like it was supposed to be played. He did it his way. It was unconventional.

What do I mean? When Bruce took a job with a bank early on in his career, he was looking forward toward a goal. He made an almost unheard of career move in those early days. He cut a deal where he only was paid a fixed percentage of whatever dollar amount he made. Now that is great if you're making money, but not so good if you're not. If you don't have a good year, you will be eating franks and beans instead of steak. That can quickly mean no steaks at The Palm, but rather 99-cent burgers at Burger King.

However, this wise deal allowed Bruce to trade as a trend following trader for the bank—to great trading size. The better he did, the more money they wanted him to trade. The more money he traded, and with continued big performance numbers, the more he made. Does that mean you will have the ability to cut a Bruce-like deal? Maybe, maybe not, but that is not the point. The true lesson is his way of *thinking*. He thought outside the box. He was making the rules three steps ahead. How many people work for a bank and create the autonomy and freedom Bruce did? Not many.

However, before you go thinking that the bank story was the secret to his success, hold tight. Bruce made his first million by the age of 30. That was his own money and his own trading—as far away from Wall Street as you could be. No excuses.

# Chapter Five

# Think Like a Poker Player and Play the Odds

*Larry Hite*

I MADE A DOCUMENTARY FILM THAT FEATURED NOBEL Prize winners, top traders, fund managers, and professional poker players. Some people questioned why poker players were in a film primarily about markets and the recent economic crisis. Unknown to many, there is a great connection between successfully trading and successfully playing poker. The winning traders and the winning poker players both think in terms of odds.

At all times when you are betting your hard-earned money, you need to think of the odds. You always want to put the odds on your side. What do I mean? Look at the lottery. People have no chance to win. The odds are stacked against them, but they still play.

Larry Hite is famous for putting the odds on his side as a trend following trader for over three decades. That means betting big money when you have a chance to win big, and not betting big when you're guaranteed to lose.

Hite is one of my favorite traders and favorite people. What makes me like him so much? More importantly how can his experience help translate to increasing your net worth?

Let's start back in the day. Hite joked about growing up. He said that he failed at blocks in kindergarten. Out of the gate, that should put his views on formal education into context. Like many rags to riches success stories, Hite grew up in the prototypical middle-class, New York-area apartment. His father owned a small business, but there were no silver spoons for his kids. Hite was blessed with learning disabilities, vision problems, and, by his own account, a short attention span. With a big smile and a touch of sarcasm, he proudly stated that those *problems* were the secret to his success. They made him a great trader.

Well, those issues really didn't cause his success, but knowing that Hite overcame many negatives is where your inspiration can start.

So how can you become a trend following winner like Hite?

Be curious! Hite first read an article about commodity trading in *Playboy*. That spurred him to go see the local winner who was working as a commodities broker in the neighborhood. This broker explained that if Hite put down $2,000, he could make $1,000 a day. Hasn't everyone heard some version of that scam? (The other day some guy e-mailed me that Mark Zuckerberg would be willing to sell me shares in Facebook right now today—before their IPO.)

These kinds of guys don't know anything about pork bellies, gold, or stocks. Even if you, like Hite in the early days, are naïve when it comes to pork bellies, you immediately know that a $2,000 investment will not make you $1,000 a day—or at least you should know that.

Hite saw another obvious contradiction. Since he was in jeans, dressing exactly how he wanted, and sleeping as late as he wanted, how could a broker who had to show up promptly at nine o'clock to work for the man make him rich?

## Irrelevant Information

It's another day at the grind and you are listening to a financial adviser pitch you on investment ideas. One broker gets up and tells you that he can be your money savior. His reasoning? When he goes to a company to talk with management he can tell you what color the CEO's eyes are.

Hite looked at that real life broker, a true story, and thought, "Geez, he's one of the stupidest people I've ever met in my life. The color of the CEO's eyes does not matter. There's no data that blue-eyed guys are better than brown-eyed guys."

You have to stay supremely focused on exactly what is relevant. What information is verifiable? What can you actually know that's not just someone's opinion? Then if it's verifiable, is it relevant? And if you have the right verified and relevant information, what follows?

You can't just take information. You have to process it and you have to think that most of the information available, like most opinion, is suspect.

---

**You don't swing at every pitch. You can wait for your perfect pitch.**

---

## Hite Gems

I have spent a great deal of time with Larry Hite. His lessons are fast, furious, and can jump from one idea to the next in quick speed. Here are some of my favorite quick gems from Hite that I know will spark Aha! moments in you and your trend following trading.

- There is a great book by Ted Williams about hitting. Williams divided the plate into sectors. He figured out there were a certain number of sectors in his strike zone, like a chessboard, and he figured out his batting average depending where the ball came across the plate. He was that detailed. He was thinking in odds. He was finding good useful information that could possibly help him to improve his batting average.

- Pretend you have a friend who made a fortune in the sanitation business. His beginnings were in a trailer park and, after hard work, he made a small fortune. Your friend decides that the silver market will go up, which it does. It goes way up, but then it starts to sink like a stone. When silver begins to fall he calls and says, "It really can't go down." You don't know. I don't know. Hite didn't know. The market is simply telling you that you are wrong.

If you have a trade that is going one way while the market is going another, how can you be right? True story—that accomplished businessman wound up living back in the same trailer park before his success.

- The first part of the winning process is evaluating who you are and what you're comfortable doing. You have to figure out what you can do. You have to ask yourself: "Who are you?" "What's important to you?"

- It doesn't stop there. Ask yourself, "Could I do this?" "Could you do it again, again, and again?" "Do you like doing it?" For example, Larry Hite likes trading systems. He doesn't just take action on a whim, he likes action to fit into context—that's the mentality he needed to be a trend following trader.

- "What do you want?" "What is the purpose of you doing this?" "What is it that you're investing in?" "Are you investing for appreciation?" "Are you investing for income?" "What is it that you want and how are you going to find yourself an unfair (legal) advantage?"

- Ask yourself another question, "When?" "When is this supposed to happen?" "What's the time frame?" "If you think something's going to happen, when is it going to happen?" The "whens" are going to tell you how much you're going to make, and what your return is going to be on a compounded basis. You have to know the answer.

- "How is it supposed to happen?" You need a goal, but in order for that goal to happen, what needs to occur for you to get from where you are today to where you want to be tomorrow?

- Nothing is more powerful in trading than compound interest. *Compound interest* is interest that accrues on the initial principal and the accumulated interest of a principal deposit, loan, or debt. Compounding of interest allows a principal amount to grow faster than *simple interest*, which is calculated as a percentage of only the principal amount.

One final important gem from Hite is that being wrong is okay. He says he was never very good in school and not much of an athlete either. But he turned that to his advantage because he was able to grasp the idea that he could be wrong. In fact, it came as no surprise to him when he was wrong.

Hite recalls with pride: "I've always built in an assumption of wrongness [in my trading]. I always ask myself: What is the worst thing that can possibly happen in this scenario? Then I use that worst-case scenario as my baseline. I always want to know what I'm risking, and how much I can lose. And sometimes, when you really look at it, there's really not all that much risk [which is why you can get rich]."

So ask yourself "What is the worst that can happen?" and go from there.

## Perfect Knowledge

―――――――――― ∼ ――――――――――

**If you're playing a positive expectation game, you don't want to be knocked out. Good stuff always takes care of itself, but you have to stay alive. You can't play if you're dead.**

―――――――――――――――――――――

Imagine you run a company with hundreds of employees. One day you walk in and say to everyone, "What is the value of perfect knowledge? What if we knew the year-ending market prices across a portfolio of markets?" Everyone would want that situation, right? Your employees would immediately all agree. Hold tight. There is more to it.

With perfect knowledge of what the prices would be on December 31 of any given year, how much leverage could you use to get maximum advantage at the beginning of that same year on January 1?

Hite found that even with perfect foresight of the ending year price you could not sustain more than three to one leverage because you can't predict the path a market might take while heading to that ending, December 31, price.

Think of it this way. GOOG is trading at 300 today on January 1, but at the end of the year, I am telling you in advance, it will be trading at 600. What would you do? Get every credit card you could and buy GOOG? Use every bit of margin in your brokerage account? Buy all the cheap options you could? After all you have perfect knowledge of the year-end price so back up the truck and load up, right? Wrong!

You can lose. How? Real simple. Even though you know the year-end price of GOOG, it could go from 300 to 50 first and then to 600. That potentially volatile up and down path can massacre your account—and if you have added leverage on top of leverage by the time it's all over you may have lost your house. See what it means to respect leverage?

---

## Follow the Leader

You've got to know the odds when you bet but there's calculation involved. Here's how to do it.

Calculating expected value is a way of measuring the positive or negative value of every bet you make.

(*Continued*)

Expected value allows you to look at your choices, or bets, objectively as opposed to emotionally. While it might seem appealing to be right 95 percent of the time, if you lose more than 20 times what you would make, you've made yourself a bad bet. By calculating the odds of winning or losing, and the amount of each outcome, you can figure out when you've got a good or bad bet on your hands.

Take a coin flip game where you win or lose the same amount every time—with 50-50 odds of coming up heads or tails in every toss. That particular bet has an expected value of zero. That's because your chance of winning is equally offset by your chance of losing. But instead of getting paid the same amount for each outcome, assume you can get paid $2 for every tail and lose $1 for each head. With a 50-50 chance of winning on each flip, but with twice the earnings payable on tails, you've now got a positive expected value game to play all day.

In its simplest form, expected value equals the amount you can win multiplied by the probability of winning minus the amount you can lose multiplied by the probability of losing. The formula looks like this:

$$EV = W \times P(W) - L \times P(L)^*$$

*Source: Stephen Fenichell and Larry Hite, "The Losers Guide to Winning," *International Creative Management*.

## Even Mentors Have Mentors

His name has come up a few times already, but amazingly, trend following pioneer Ed Seykota reappears. Seykota was one of the first to trade "across the board"—meaning he traded all markets in a similar fashion with a system.

Hite shared a story: "Seykota had a trend following system and one day his boss came to him and said, 'Ed, you don't have a potato trade.' And he said, 'Yeah, my system doesn't have a potato trade.' Three days later his boss came back to him again and said, 'Look, Ed, you've not recommended a potato trade . . . do you hear me?' And Seykota said, 'My system doesn't have a potato trade.' And the boss said, 'Look, we have a trading desk on the potato trading floor. You have to recommend for the whole trading floor. How is this going to look that you don't have a potato trade?'"

This went on for about a month until Seykota left the firm. Like today, with many brokers and talking heads, his boss could have cared less that there was no trade to take. They wanted to fill in the blanks and give their clients something—even if it was worthless trading advice. Sound familiar?*

*Larry Hite speech, February 7, 2003.

A big lesson: Focus on what is important, not the extraneous. Extraneous is trying to create a trade out of nothing just to have a trade.

Trend following trading is not about being a hero. Said another way, it is not about being right in your opinion, but rather about winning in the long run. Some people just want to be perceived superstars, like reality TV wannabes, but that is not what you want to be.

You want to be practical. For example, how much are you willing to lose? You can say, "I'm willing to lose 5 percent of my capital or 100 percent of my capital," but you have to know the number.

Yes, you are going to be a trend follower and yes, you are going to be looking for trends, but you can't predict those trends, their duration, or their timing. That said you have to give yourself leeway so you can survive the inevitable downturns or bad times. That's why you need to know what kind of loss you are talking about.

## Dating Game

Here is a great (and funny) story about the ability to win by properly thinking in terms of odds. You are a young guy. You are a freshman in college. What are you thinking about? One thing: girls. How do you meet them?

How do you get one? Hite has the solution for all guys unlucky in love—and it's all about numbers.

Imagine leaving the house routinely. You see the same guy pass you, always with a fabulous-looking woman—not necessarily the same one—yet you walk alone.

One day you say to the other guy, "Excuse me." You ask how he meets the beautiful women parading by on his arm: "Where do you find all of these good-looking girls?" And he says, "Not a problem."

He says, "Look, it's really very simple. Whenever I see a really attractive girl I go over and say, 'Hi, my name is Harry. I'd like to buy you a cup of coffee.'" He added, "One out of 10 will go for coffee with me. One out of the 10 that go for coffee will end up being more serious."

Hite thought that this was one of the greatest examples of thinking in odds that he had ever heard because it involved the two things that he was most interested in—probabilities and the opposite sex.

Not only is this story about numbers and odds, the more people you meet the better chance you have, but it is also about rejection (read: loss). Can you stand to be rejected? Can you stand to lose?

Which brings us back to risk.

Nine times out of 10 is how often you are going to lose with that dating technique, but it comes down to the simple question, "Is the risk worth the reward?" For many, whether those looking to date or looking to trade, the risk is certainly worth the reward.

---

**A soldier came back from Vietnam and said, "There are two kinds of helicopter pilots. There are old pilots and bold pilots, but there are no old bold pilots."**

---

The trading game is about bets and Hite is clear about that: "There are four kinds of bets. There are bets you win and bets you lose. There are good bets and bad bets. You can win on a bad bet. You can lose on a good bet, but the point is you do a lot better on good bets."

Ask yourself, "What's a good bet and are you regularly taking them?"

## How Much Can You Lose?

It starts with what can you tolerate: "How much money are you willing to lose on a trade?" You want to let the market have room to go within your preset stop parameters. You are always in control of this, and you always know what you are doing—no matter what happens. You are making sure that you are as prepared as possible.

You can't be totally prepared because that is impossible (i.e., a meteor wiped out the dinosaurs, for example), but you can be prepared enough to handle whatever problems may arise in your trading, and handle them correctly (read: Get out when your stop is hit).

If Alan Greenspan and Ben Bernanke could be fooled by the economic crisis, what would stop Hite (or you) from being fooled as well? Nothing. But at least Hite knows that. He starts from an assumed position of ignorance. You have to be realistic. But you don't actually have to do anything. You can go broke by ignoring this wisdom too.

You have to know that you don't know. No matter what information you have, no matter what you are doing, you can be wrong. A friend of Hite's, who amassed a fortune in excess of $100 million, passed on prescient lessons: If you never bet your lifestyle, from a trading standpoint, nothing bad will ever happen to you, and if you know what the worst possible outcome is from the outset, you will have tremendous freedom. Freedom from what, you say? Stress for starters!

The simple and time immemorial truth is that while you can't quantify reward (no one knows when the big trend will come and no one knows how big it will be), you can quantify risk. Non-academic version? You alone control how much of your limited supply of money (and we all have some version of a limited supply) you are willing to lose.

A constant principle within Hite's trading: Never risk more than 1 percent of your total account on any one trade. If you only risk 1 percent, you are indifferent to any individual trade, and more importantly it can't kill you.

I want you to have one major *numero uno* takeaway from Larry Hite: You don't trade markets. You trade *money*.

---

**Hite has two basic rules about trading and life:**
**1) If you don't bet, you can't win.**
**2) If you lose all your chips, you can't bet.**

---

## The Backstory

Larry Hite is a legend. I did not lead with the details of his career on purpose. I wanted you to see his wisdom and find an Easter egg at the end of this chapter—namely the severe credibility upon which his wisdom is based.

Hite is without a doubt one of the founding fathers of systematic trend following trading. He founded Mint Investments in 1981 and by 1990 it was the largest trend following fund in the world. Hite later formed a partnership with Man Group. Man soon bought AHL, another trend follower named after its three founders: Michael Adam, David Harding (see Harding next chapter) and Martin Lueck. Today, Man Investments is the largest trend firm in the world by a country mile. Much of this success chain traces back to Hite. Recently, Hite partnered up with his longtime Man colleague, Stanley Fink.

When asked how he came to the decision to join International Standard Asset Management (ISAM), Hite painted a lesson: "Many years ago, I had a client, a gentleman in the baked-goods industry, who came to me after having sold off his business for $10 million. In discussing his investment options, I told him this kind of thing doesn't happen often, and he corrected me, explaining that he had indeed done this very type of deal several times. He went on to explain that he had an incredibly simple formula for success. First, he kept to an industry he knew very well, which was bakeries, obviously, and second, he only partnered with men in their mid-thirties. This was young enough to have energy and youth, he pointed out, but old enough to be tempered by experience. I could immediately see the beauty of this fellow's philosophy, and I always kept it at the forefront of my mind when I considered ventures of my own."*

*Harriet Agnew, "Managed Futures: It's the Hite Club," *Financial News*, February 28, 2011. See: www.efinancialnews.com/story/2011-02-28/managed-futures.

# Chapter Six

# Stand Up, Dust Yourself Off, and Keep Going

—≈—

*David Harding*

WHO DOESN'T WANT TO MAKE A BILLION DOLLARS? YES, I imagine there are downsides to that type of wealth, but it must be one helluva ride to produce that kind of success—especially from essentially nothing. Is it a reasonable goal for you to make a billion dollars? Well, the odds are probably not on your side for that.

However, sometimes in this world, this crazy and often chaotic world of ours, people win the lottery. They buy a scratch-off ticket and win millions. They didn't practice. They didn't struggle. They didn't do anything except buy a scratch-off ticket.

On the other side are people like David Harding. Harding struggled mightily early. However, Harding stuck with it for decades and is now a true billionaire. Don't get me wrong—Harding, like many success stories, has had luck on his side.

However, that's not the takeaway here. The takeaway is perseverance. The takeaway is not quitting. That's how Harding really hit it big. Without perseverance, Harding would have had no chance for luck to shine through.

What can you do? You can learn to think like a trader who has made a billion dollars. And if you think like him, and if you model how a trader like that views the world, you can put yourself in a place to possibly make your billion. Note, I said *possibly*. The real reason, the honest reason to think like a billionaire, is to make your first million. Anyone with guts and determination can figure a way to make their first million, but you have to stick with the ups and downs.

Known as the commodities king (primarily because the press always talk about some of the markets trend followers trade as opposed to their strategy), London's Harding could be called an overnight trading sensation—only 30 years in the making.

His trend following trading has produced, on average, nearly 20 percent a year for 20 years. Let that digest for a second as you ponder the buy and hold investments in mutual funds you may have, slowing eating away at your capital and your sanity.

These days, the white-haired financial wizard (still under 50) enjoys collecting books on economic history, some dating back to the 1860s. In my time with him, he carried that distinct American entrepreneurial spirit center stage, along with a salty tongue of randy one-liners, all wrapped in a quintessential British flair.*

## It All Starts with the Tedious Grind

Harding is bright. No doubt. He graduated with a degree in physics from Cambridge University, but without the requisite hard work, a degree like that doesn't make him a trend following winner today. Plus, last I checked, physics is physics. It was not a degree in trend following.

Early on, Harding devoured *technical analysis* books and saw the benefits of trend following, but he quickly realized that he wanted scientific analysis in his trading.

*Colin Fernandez, "Rambler with an Interest in Bible Studies Is the City's Highest Earner at $60 Million a Year," September 27, 2010. See: www.dailymail.co.uk/news/article-1315366/David-Harding-Citys-highest-earner-60m-year.html.

He originally started at someone else's firm to learn. "I went there because I didn't want to sit in an investment bank and make money. I wanted to know if you could do [trend following] from outside the markets looking in. 'Could you be on a desert island and make money trading?' [That] was the question I was asking myself."*

That kind of question was only going to be answered through hard work. Imagine yourself spending every day drawing hundreds of charts by hand. Harding did. He bound every chart into big leather folders. It became his leather bound book of charts so to speak. Why do this? Research! If you believe that all markets can be made the same through the analysis of their price movements, then you have to prove it to yourself too. You have to do the homework by staring at the price data and staring at the charts.

Harding added, "The only thing I ever wanted to be was a quantitative trader, because I think like that. Just like a violinist needs to play a violin, I need to take a quantitative approach to markets. I'm only interested in the maths."† ("Maths" is the very British way to say it.)

---

*Simon Kerr, "Winton Capital Management: Simon Kerr Talks to David Harding," *The Hedge Fund Journal*, September 2005. See: www.thehedge fundjournal.com/magazine/200509/interviews/simon-kerr-talks-to-david-harding.php.
†Ibid.

This is not new, however. Investment success and maths have been hand-in-hand for centuries. It is not something that just happened suddenly in the late twentieth century. Today may be a golden era for the two to work together with the explosion of computers and globalization, but using rules that allow you to count is anything but new when it comes to making money.

The two great waves of our time opened up huge opportunities for traders to do clever things. Investing globally around the world with math and computers, and pursuing more trend trading strategies, are just a few of the advantages.

Think about it. If you are looking at many markets, and you have rules that require constant recalculating and monitoring, is it really a shock that there are many more opportunities to make money in global markets as opposed to just 20 years ago? Said another more pedestrian way: Trend following is the only style of trading that you can operate out of your bedroom. It is the only style of trading that doesn't require you to stare at a monitor all day. Those are not small differentiating factors!

## Don't Get Caught Up in Labels

The trend following approach to markets is really a science. It is an unpublished science, but it is a real one. Harding was clear, "You could get the thick leather bound volumes of papers on it if there was a willingness to open the kimono, as the horrible modern expression has it."*

He trades everything using trend following systems, and it works. By simulation, he can come up with ideas and hypotheses, and test those—just like other traders we have seen so far. Over the years, what he has done, essentially, is conduct trend trading experiments. But instead of using a microscope or a telescope, his computer is his laboratory instrument. And instead of looking at the stars, he is looking at data and simulation languages.[†]

---

~

**Trend trading strategies take money and turn it into more money. It's a pretty simple principle.**

---

When looking at market data there are many different charts, versions of charts, and indicators. So what exactly is the relevant data to look at? Price data. You can trade futures, exchange traded funds (ETFs), and a host of

---

*Ibid.

[†]Geoffrey Newman, "Intuition and Hard Facts are Behind Winton's Success," *Business*, September 10, 2008. See: www.theaustralian.com.au/business/wealth/intuition-and-the-hard-facts/story-e6frgad6-1111117404721.

different instruments as a trend following trader using price data alone. That said, many trend followers trade futures contracts because they are a liquid, cheap, and effective way to trade on a global basis.

While it is not relevant to your personal trend following trading, it is relevant to know how professional trend followers are labeled if you plan to invest with a trend following firm.

Many are described as CTAs, which means Commodity Trading Advisor. It is a regulatory category in the United States. However, it is a major misnomer since trend followers don't trade only commodities. They trade everything from stocks to currencies to cotton to Swiss francs to cocoa.

Many trend following firms are also labeled as managed futures traders, which is another confusing misnomer. That term, like CTA, doesn't describe the trading strategy style either—it refers back to the instrument being traded.

Harding is not dogmatic about describing himself as anything, but finds it to be a necessity for clients. Clients take comfort in fitting him into a box. He finds boxes are better than nothing, and with a wide smile he offered: "Otherwise, we'd be miscellaneous and who would want to be miscellaneous?"

## Trader's Kryptonite

Harding's initial research decades ago led to a simple conclusion: Trend-trading systems worked, or at least back then he found that they had worked. Of course it's not enough to say that, because something has worked, it will go on working, but Harding noted that it is a matter of record that trend following has gone on working for a long enough time for him to set up two very large and successful firms centered around trend following.*

At the root of these successful firms, and at the root of your potential trading success, is a relatively straight-forward concept: control risk. It can't be said enough. To not respect risk is Kryptonite for all traders.

A definition of risk is uncertainty of outcome. Risk means that you can't control the end result of a particular situation, but if you take on a gamble, the risk has to be worth the perceived reward. Risk, however, is not specific to investment markets. Risk is something that everybody takes on every day. We all face risks from all angles at all times.

Every time you drive a car, every time you fly in an airplane, you are taking a risk. You calculate that risk.

*David Harding interview, *Hedge Funds Review*, May 20, 2010. See: www .hedgefundsreview.com/hedge-funds-review/news/1649591/video-interview-david-harding-founder-managing-director-winton-capital-management.

You know there is a one in a million chance, for example, that when you go on a car trip, you are going to die. You don't, however, let that stand in the way of going to visit your sister. Or do you?!

We all take risks and have become perfectly comfortable with risk to achieve a desired outcome. But there is always a small amount of uncertainty in that outcome as with all human activities. All activities, trend following included, have uncertainty in outcome.

For example, the nature of risk is apparent in the field of medicine, for when you get a disease the conversation with a doctor can quickly turn to a conversation about mortality. You may die earlier than you otherwise would have as a result of indulging in some risky activity—skiing, for example.

People take different risks. Some sky dive, some fly, some smoke, and some travel. Some take much greater risks than others, for some higher reward, but it is all still risk taking.

Others, like the elderly gentlemen on the park bench, probably figure that he doesn't need additional risk and will happily see out his last few years avoiding it, feeding the pigeons, and playing with his grandkids.

Because people have different desires and attitudes toward risk taking, it has to be assessed differently for each individual. Everyone takes risk in investing and trading, but the differentiating factor is that very few attempt to estimate their risk choices with mathematical tools.

For example, some blindly move their money into investments with heavy, but undefined, risk on the line. You should never participate in a game where you have not accurately assessed your downside. Accurately measuring the risks you are taking can insure that you are taking wise risks, those right for you and your lifestyle.

Once you have that foundational thinking, it carries over to the markets seamlessly. What is the major uncertainty of outcome across the spectrum of investments for everybody? Trying to acquire a vast amount of wealth!

Between 95 and 99 percent of the human population is interested on some level in acquiring more wealth. Some desperately want to be very rich. Some just want a little bit more money, perhaps to buy a slightly better house or a new car. Some just want to save for security.

Clearly, people are eager to pursue more ways of acquiring more wealth, but there is no way to acquire more real wealth without taking risk. Even putting your money in the bank is not a zero risk because the value of your money changes over time (read: inflation).

And there are ways of measuring risk. There are ways of quantifying it. They might all be deeply imperfect, but there are ways to start measuring it. However, you don't want to make the mistake of being blinded by science.

The old saying, "A little knowledge is a dangerous thing" rings true. For example, some calculate risk as standard deviation of return.

*Standard deviation* is a statistical measurement that sheds light on historical volatility. It shows how much variation or "dispersion" there is from the "average." For example, a volatile stock may have a high standard deviation while the deviation of a stable blue chip stock may be lower. A large dispersion tells how much a return is deviating from the expected normal returns.

But standard deviation is not the way to properly measure and/or assess risk—especially if you are a trend following trader. Why?

As a trend following trader you will make your money far outside the bounds of normality. This means you will make your big money in the "tail" of the bell curve.

What constitutes as "far outside the bounds of normality?" When a portfolio is put together, it is generally assumed that the distribution of returns will follow a normal pattern. Under this assumption, the probability that returns will move between the mean and three standard deviations, either positive or negative, is 99.97 percent. This means that the probability of returns moving more than three standard deviations beyond the mean is 0.03 percent, or virtually nil. However, the concept of tail risk suggests that the distribution is not normal, but skewed, and has fatter tails. The fatter tails increase the probability that an investment will move beyond three standard deviations. Distributions that are characterized by *fat tails* are what we see when we look at trend following returns.

Okay, I know that is a mini-class on statistics, but what do you want? Do you want to gripe or do you want to make money?

---

**Don't get caught up constantly trying to lower your risks. Think of yourself as running a risk targeting business where you go *find* risk. No risk, no reward!**

---

## Conventional Wisdom

It is generally accepted that if you invest money in a well-diversified portfolio of stocks, and hold them forever, that you will do quite well. But how many people do that? Occasionally somebody dies, some widow who is 93, and relatives learn that she is worth $48 million because she's done exactly that—hold on forever. She bought some stocks available to her when she was young, she didn't watch CNBC, and at the end of a lifetime she dies unknowingly loaded. Sound like a plan for you? Not really.

CNBC is for people who want to do things more actively and that's not a blessing. Being more active in your investing or trading is a curse, especially if you don't know what you are doing. The chances of someone knowing the bare minimum of trading, and watching CNBC for success, is probably less than 1 percent. Real successful traders don't watch the news for the their decision making cues.

If you're an outsider, not working at J.P. Morgan for example, and you are trying to be an active trader, a day trader, a swing trader, someone watching tick by tick all day long, then you are up against a big hurdle trying to beat professionals. You might have confidence to believe that you can beat professionals, but are you really cleverer than everybody else?

This idea that you can beat the pros as an active trader by following the news will be an expensive proposition—guaranteed. You may indeed be cleverer than average, but you've got to be quite a lot cleverer than average. There are many great, clever people out there and they spend their lives 24/7 working to extricate profits from the markets. At least with a trend following philosophy you have a chance.

Harding was struck by the curious fact that interest rates in the United States are set by a so-called high priest of government. Market forces are not the driver.

## Follow the Leader

Take it from David Harding: Outcomes, or what actually happens, don't tell you very much. The process is what is so important.

But of course, most people draw their conclusions from outcomes. They see what happens and they say, "Oh, that's what happened and therefore, I can draw this or that conclusion." You could almost label that way of thinking as superstitious, but it's erroneous; it's wrong. You don't want to make decisions for the wrong reasons. If you're going to make the wrong decisions for the wrong reasons, then it's not going to be good for increasing your wealth.

## Not the Art, the Science of Trading

I have seen it for years. People want to debate the success and viability of trend following trading. They complain that it's just a theory and that any type of theory can neither be true or false. Of course, all theories are conditionally true and every scientist knows in his heart of hearts that what measures the interestingness of scientific theory is utility; how useful it is, how interesting it is, and whether it gives an interesting insight. There are lots and lots of possible theories that lay out boring predicates that no one is interested in.

Now if a theory makes an interesting prediction, like the orbit of Mercury will be slightly different from where it appears to be, or where it would be with Newtonian mechanics, that captures attention. If it's true, that's testable, and if it's true, then you could split the atom.

There is a huge consequence from that story. It's all terribly interesting and the interestingness was obvious to everybody. The minute it was done, it was on the front page of the *New York Times*. Even though nobody understood relativity, everyone understood the significance of it. It's not controversial. People intuitively understood the measure of a scientific theory in that example, its utility and usefulness.

Harding ran with that foundation. "I think the efficient market hypothesis is quite useful too. One prediction it makes is that it is difficult to beat the markets. It's just saying that the market knows better than you do. So the assumption that the market knows better than you do is quite a sensible and useful assumption. It certainly would lead you to approach [beating the markets] with humility and modesty."

Warren Buffett compares playing in the markets against people who believe in the efficient market hypothesis to playing bridge against people who don't believe in looking at their cards.

In other words, clearly with your speculator's hat on, you want to be playing against others who don't believe at looking at their cards, or playing against opponents who believe in efficient market hypothesis. That's a good trading direction to take if you want the chance for wealth.

I don't know how anyone can argue against the notion that the success of systematic trend following trading is a living and breathing, profit making refutation of efficient market hypothesis.

## Stay Humble

Even though Harding has been very frank, there is some reticence. He knows talking too much about trend following is a retrograde step for his business's commercial prospects.

Why would a competitive man want to encourage you to become the next billionaire? He doesn't have a mission to spread trend following wisdom or propagate this style of trading. He is not interested in sponsoring academic trend following courses or making the world a better place filled with wealthy trend following traders. He is entrepreneurial man who, after all, wants to win.

---

### Follow the Leader

Leaders don't forget that investing is a betting game. Investing is a form of gambling; it is betting. They are both intellectually similar activities, but of course you should have no interest in playing a game where, according to the laws of the game, you cannot win.

If a game has a payout ratio of less than one—and gambling games have a payout ratio of less than one—it means the longer you play, the more certain you are to lose. In any game, once you know that, there should be no interest. However, for some it is just that fact that pushes them to play more. They want to beat the odds. Prove everyone wrong. Unfortunately, the house wants to win more than you, and the house can always last longer than you and your money. Oh sure, maybe you occasionally gamble for pleasure and it can be rational for people to gamble knowing that they're going to lose for the pleasure of it alone. Some get a lot of pleasure from the small probability of a very large win. They get far more pleasure from that small probability than the chance they will ever win the huge money. If you're essentially doing something irrational, it doesn't mean your behavior is irrational because, in theory, you are not doing it for primary financial reasons. Now, if you are doing it for financial reasons . . . trouble ahead!

## Entrepreneurism

For those lucky enough to study Latin in their youth, you recall the verb "speculari," which translates as "to observe."

Speculators, while often vilified in the press, are observers, which is very much the position you want to find yourself in as you go about making money in the markets. You want to stand outside of the political and economic system (chaos!) and observe. The best defense that can be made of people profiting from speculation is George Soros's defense: You are playing a game that anyone can play and you play by the rules laid down.

However, once you accept speculation as an accepted direction, *determination* enters the arena for everyone's potential success. Harding's grandmother used to say "Patience and perseverance made a bishop of his reverence."

Harding opined, "Determination is the same as having wings. If at first you don't succeed, try, try, and try again. Madonna always says, 'I'm like a cockroach.'"

Meaning, no one could kill Madonna.

You have to take those views to heart, especially during tough times. You might ask, "Once you've made enough money, why keep persevering?"

In Europe many would say that if you've made enough money, however much that may be, you should go do something worthwhile with your life. It's a slightly more American notion to climb to the top because it's there. It used to be more English, but now it's more American to go and conquer "it" because it's there.

Harding sees that philosophy as a fantastic tradition that only exists in America. When he was 20 and living in the United States, he read Ayn Rand. He was struck by her politics and economics, not because he is a lifelong convert, but because he didn't see her kind of entrepreneurial writing in Europe. He didn't see those ideas there.

Harding was also influenced by another precept: You have been given abilities and it is your duty to make use of them. Religious people make that argument. They say if God has given you abilities, then it is your duty to use them.

That is not necessarily easy since fear of failure is a very real factor for many, but you can be driven by fear of failure to some extent. It can bring out the competition in you.

Everyone has something in the world they are good at. Harding's talent is analyzing distribution of the financial price dynamics (fancy way of saying trend following). And he has been doing it for 20-plus years. He makes really good money at it. Consequently, he believes it is God's way of telling him to do more of it.

*Chapter Seven*

# Throw Away the Fundamentals and Stick to Your Charts

— ∾ —

*Bernard Drury*

WE'VE ALL BEEN TRAINED TO EXPECT STORIES. THE MOST commonly asked question by investors is: "Where is the market going?" People want a prediction. They want to hear a story that will give them the edge needed to beat out their neighbor in the markets. Following the forecast of how many iPhones will be sold next year, if the Brazilian coffee crop will be as expected or not, or if the Fed will influence interest rates—is not the way to make big money. Bernard Drury is a great example of a trader who, early in his career, followed that way of thinking. Only later did he come to the realization that trend following was a more direct path. He let go of fundamentals. For that reason alone he shows that you can change the way you view the world—even if you have been set in your ways for decades.

Drury graduated cum laude from Dartmouth College with a degree in Russian. His trading career began in 1978 as a grain trader for the Louis Dreyfus Corporation. Drury spent the next 15 years as a commercial grain trader, grain market researcher, and proprietary trader for his own account. He was all about understanding, and then trading based on fundamentals.*

What exactly do grain trader and researcher mean? Here is an excerpt from Reuters, which gives an example of using fundamental analysis in the grain markets:

> U.S. grain markets will get their direction this week from old-fashioned supply-and-demand fundamentals after being pushed around recently by outside influences such as movements in the U.S. dollar and the price of crude oil. The U.S.

*"Monthly Performance Report," Drury Capital Incorporated, October 2008, 3.

Department of Agriculture is due to release its estimate of corn and soybean crops on Tuesday morning. It will provide the market with plenty of data to chew on and should drive price movement throughout the week. The government also will provide its first estimate of how much winter wheat acreage was seeded in the United States last autumn. Another key for the grains markets will be weather in South America, where farmers in Brazil and Argentina are harvesting soybean crops. Analysts were expecting U.S. corn production to fall from earlier forecasts as harvest delays and wintry conditions forced Midwest farmers to shut down harvest operations before the cutting was completed. An average of estimates pegged the corn crop at 12.821 billion bushels, down 100 million from the government's December forecast. Snowstorms across the Midwest during the past week contributed to the light sales on the cash market as most farmers did not want to brave icy roads to deliver supplies to elevators and processors.

That stuff never ends. There is so much of it online you could lose your mind trying to keep track of it all. That's what it means to be a fundamental grain trader.

Does that sound like something you could do? If you think you could, how long would it take you to assemble all of that expertise? How many years of your life would go by? And even if you were smart and studious enough, would having all of the expertise to translate fundamentals allow you to know the right time to buy or sell in the markets to make money in the long run?

That's the conundrum you face. You don't want to get caught up in the idea of using fundamental analysis to trade grains, corn, wheat, and all other markets. That applies to Intel or the U.S. dollar. Same point. Lots and lots of data, but with no guarantee at all that the fundamental analysis would actually make money.

## The Traditional Way

I met Drury at the Yale Club in New York City. Being a suburban kid from the Northern Virginia area, I am still not sure what goes on at the Yale Club, but it is where I first began to understand the unique trading education that Drury's experience could impart.

His early fundamentally driven ambitions reflected what he saw as the best potential success that he could reasonably achieve in the markets. He saw traders around him who were 10, 15, and 20 years older. He was well aware that these were some very successful, wealthy, and prominent grain speculators and they were all using fundamentals to make money.

Consequently, Drury was rigorous with his fundamental studies.

He spent 20 years accumulating fundamental expertise in grain markets. He developed great respect for those traders who were sector specialists. However, while pursuing an executive MBA at the University of Chicago, his studies with Professor Robin Hogarth in the area of decision making amidst uncertainty had a lasting influence.

While in his MBA program, Drury took a class on modeling and became even more interested in quantitative, research-based approaches to trading (read: trend following). Drury explains: "I entered that U of Chicago program as a grain trader, but I already was accustomed to creating and applying econometric models to evaluate grain pricing situations. The studies with Professor Hogarth increased my curiosity about the ways in which models, or expert systems, could be applied to situations such as trading."*

## The Switch

Imagine you are a really good trader who trades only one market. You trade corn. Or maybe you trade GE. Maybe you trade silver. The big problem: Applying principles of diversification is very difficult with one market alone.

---

*"Alternative Market Briefing," *Opalesque*, November 11, 2008. See: www .opalesque.com/AMBarchive/Newsletter_BB_11112008.html.

After school, and early in his fund management career, Drury was trading $25 million in client money. However, he was having major problems with futures markets and their position and liquidity limits. He was becoming too much a part of the market in assorted grains. Meaning, the market was no longer big enough for him to trade smartly, and his concentrated trading was part of his problem.

But there was a larger issue at play. If you are a sector specialist, taking advantage of infrequent, but very important, price moves that may occur in a given market—not just grains—is very hard. Technical trend trading systems are much better at dealing with the major outright price moves.*

It was time for a change. Diversification was becoming a necessity.

That said, an evolution from a single market specialist to systematic trend trading was not overnight for Drury. First, he joined Commodities Corporation (CC) in 1994 as part of its trader program.

Commodities Corporation was a trading firm, and trading incubator, based in Princeton, New Jersey, that was particularly noted for their trend following trading.

---

*"Monthly Performance Report," Drury Capital Incorporated, October 2008, 3.

CC launched the careers of many notable traders—such as Michael Marcus, Bruce Kovner, Ed Seykota, and Paul Tudor Jones. Goldman Sachs bought CC in 1997.

Commodities Corporation started as a fundamentally driven trading firm too, but eventually they came to realize that trend following trading was the real breadwinner.

Drury operated independently under the CC umbrella (see more in my book, *The Complete Turtle Trader*). But it was a bull market in the grains in 1995 and 1996 that led Drury to finally shift away from fundamentals to a 100 percent systematic trend following strategy.

Those huge bull markets in wheat and corn, for example, could not have been successfully traded by fundamentals alone. He saw that. He lived it.

A further trigger to 100 percent trend following came in the form of Ed Seykota (whom he met through Commodities Corporation). Seykota compelled him to do more research in the technical trading area.

> I made the decision that I would give up the use of my experience as a sector specialist in favor of adopting a systematic approach in which the most important benefits are the application of very extensive research, consistency of method, and diversification.

He continued,

> For example, if we are curious about a trading rule, we run a simulation across a portfolio of about 70 instruments and 15 years of data. If we run a simulation on three or four systems together, then we get an even more robust result. This type of research provides some benefits that are difficult for a discretionary or fundamental trader to have.*

## Follow the Leader

There are different decision-making frameworks between fundamental and trend following traders, and you need to understand what yours is.

In the past Drury could talk about grain markets all day long, as that was his passion. When Drury was a fundamental trader he would talk about value extensively. For example, if the corn market was at $2.25 and you thought it could go up, you might formulate something such as: the price could go down $0.15 and it could go up $0.60. That's an attractive risk to reward so you would put on a

---

*Bernard Drury, "2010 New York Round Table," *Opalesque*.

position. But if it goes half that distance what do you do next? The risk-reward has shifted greatly. There is probably new information that is supporting your original hypothesis, but the risk-reward has shifted. A prudent trader who is operating on a value premise might reasonably exit or lighten up based on these shifted odds. By contrast, a technical trader who is following price action may act very differently. A fundamental trader might call the beginning of a trend right, when he perceives a value opportunity, but will often have difficulty taking advantage of pronounced trends. In other words, the same market information can lead to drastically different trading actions, because of different decision-making frameworks between fundamental and trend following traders. From a risk standpoint the fundamental trader is actually taking on risk by giving up on the potential big trends. By trying to be so risk averse, the fundamental trader actually is taking on more risk.

*Source:* Bernard Drury, "2010 New York Round Table," *Opalesque.*

## Drury's Core Principles

I want you to see some of the detail that drives Drury's current trend following trading. These bullets, like ones seen in Chapters 3 and 5, give concrete precepts worth emblazing across your daily trend following life:*

- Don't have a discretionary reaction to your draw-downs (meaning when you are on a losing streak). Your new position sizing (how much is right to bet on each trade) is always calculated based on your daily account value, so the size of your new positions will decline when your account value drops.
- Decide to be in or out of each market. Out of 30 traded markets, for example, you might be positioned in each market about two-thirds of the time, and out of the market about one-third of the time. Those are rough guides as it often all depends on whether markets are moving.
- Over multi-year periods when (in simulation) a given sector or group of markets does well for a time, it will be followed by poor results for a time. There is an ebb and flow, but unlike with the tides, there is no way to predict trends.
- Calculate the risk on your trade prior to entering your trade. Simple enough, but often ignored. Trading position size needs to reflect the volatility of the market at the time of your entry.

*E-mail correspondence with Bernard Drury.

- A portfolio should be broadly diversified, including approximately half of your total trades in financial markets (interest rates, currencies, and stocks) and half of your total trades in physical commodities. You want to enter into incipient trends, exit with discipline when those trends fail, and remain with winning trends for long periods. Drury primarily trades with futures markets, but you can consider exchange traded funds (ETFs) too.

## CNBC Interview

One of the best ways you can learn trend following is to look at the performance track records including annual *rate of return* for professional trend following traders (many are listed at the end of this book in Appendix A). It is proof. It is confidence for your own trading. For example, Drury's strategy made 75.65 percent during the crisis year of 2008. That is not a mutual fund return.

Early in 2008 many trend followers had long positions in crude oil as it moved up close to $150 a barrel. At the time metals and grain markets were also strong, but nearly all markets began to reverse in late July and early August. Many trend followers, including Drury, exited from long positions and eventually went short—betting to make money as markets headed down. Remember, up and down you can make money.

During his 2008 success Drury gave a rare interview on CNBC.* The CNBC host wanted to know how Drury did "it." A simple sounding but loaded question if there ever was one!

In his answer he brought it back to the price data. He applied his trend following model to the price data, and without having any insight as whether crude oil would go up or down or sideways, he was looking for certain price configurations. Drury got his entry signal in oil, and went short. Did he know crude oil was going to go up to $150? No. Did he know it was going to fall to $60? No. But the pendulum swings both ways, so he wanted to be along for the trend ride.

No trend following model is clairvoyant. Nothing and no one can predict what direction crude oil will take next month or next year. As a trend following trader you try to exploit trends for as long as they may continue, and you must work with what the present price data is telling you to do in the context of your trading system. That means living in the moment of *now*.

## Crisis Times

Yes, I know, and Bernard Drury knows, that this approach to trading often has very successful runs when others are

*CNBC Reports*, interview with Bernard Drury, November 13, 2008.

headed to the poorhouse with an inferior trading strategy. When the next crisis time happens, such as in 2008, trend trading will produce trading opportunities—huge ones at that! That is a much better option than just buying gold. When you are a technical trend trader, and you are applying very strict risk rules to your portfolio, you have a chance to make money during downward spirals. You don't have to just sit there and take it.

How does that translate? Consider current fears of a bond market collapse or hyperinflation. Could it happen? Sure. Or it might be disinflationary forces that carry the day, with interest rates remaining low and bond markets staying strong. In either event, your process for managing your trend following portfolio must be grounded in rules that allow you to win no matter what happens. You can't be guessing.*

Worse yet, consider an underlying premise of many hedge fund strategies (the ones touted in the press so often): mean reversion. Mean reversion is when a trader believes he has found a mispricing in an extended market and expects a return to *normal* prices (whatever normal is). This is exactly what many hedge funds do. It never works in the long run. That kind of thinking blows up with regularity.

*E-mail correspondence with Bernard Drury.

As a trend follower you do just the opposite. You look for directional moves (read: trends) to persist. Don't make it more complicated than that.

## Winners Always Adjust

What's so interesting about Drury is the real education you can take away from his career that can help you to make money. He began with fundamental trading. Not just in college, or for a year or two after college. He traded as a fundamental grain trader for 15-plus years. He led a very narrow trading life focused very specifically on one group of markets, and after 15 years he figured out that it wasn't too late to convert. He arrived at his trend following understanding in a much different manner than most every trend following trader that I have learned from—and that's quite a few. Lesson: There simply is no singular path to systematic trend trading success.

All of us are afforded new information every day of our lives. The issue is not if you are lucky enough to be exposed to trend following in this book; the issue is what will you do now that you know about trend following?

*Chapter Eight*

# Study Hard and Get an A+

## *Justin Vandergrift*

---

THERE IS ONLY ONE FACTOR THAT YOU CAN CONTROL WHEN you start trading: how much you are willing to lose. You cannot control how much you will make. You cannot project that desire no matter your good intentions or happy thoughts. You can only stop, for sure, a losing trade. That is in your power. The great traders understand that you must know how much you can lose at all times. That is the essence of risk management. It is the essence of Justin

Vandergrift's progression to becoming a successful trend following trader. His story and lessons are yet another inspirational and confidence building example that you can take to your own trading. Study up and succeed.

Trading calls some at an early age. Imagine you are 10 years old and your great uncle begins teaching you about stocks. At about 15, your dad shows you futures trading (he is trading the sugar market). Immediate fascination grabs your mind.

You thought sugar was something you bought in five-pound bags at the grocery store, not a market that could be traded for profit? Who wakes up and thinks that you can buy and sell something like sugar to make money, even if you have no need for the sugar? I know I didn't years ago.

Vandergrift spent his teen years drawing market charts on grid paper (this was before computer charting). Being close to the numbers created an intimate connection, something lost now with computer charting and all the fancy software packages. (Gary Davis in Chapter 1 made the same point.)

It was not long before Vandergrift was taking odd jobs, like bagging groceries and other menial tasks, just to save money to trade sugar through his dad's account. It was not all roses. He learned the harsh lesson early on that trading has ups and downs. Losing hurts; therefore, how do you find a way to win?

After all, winning is everything in the trading game. That is the same mentality most of us have when we are growing up. Everyone usually wants to win. I played baseball in college. I was very competitive. Always wanted to win. Is everyone into sports? No.

Vandergrift was the youngest in his class. He graduated from high school at the age of 17. Not only was he the youngest in his class, he was undersized. How did that motivate him? How did that drive his sense of competitiveness? He knew the only way to win would be in the classroom rather than the playing field. He figured 9 out of the 10 "high school jocks" (his derogatory reference!) would not amount to much on the financial playground, and that was where he intended to thrive. Most athletes think the only type of drive that matters happens on a playing field. In actuality, many of the most competitive people never step foot on a field, but it does not mean there is any less will to win.

I do not care what you do in your life, trading or whatever, that drive to win, that drive to excel, that drive to beat the competition had better be there. If not, take a job working for the man and take what your buy-and-hope mutual fund has to offer. Life will be much more secure and vanilla that way.

Starting Out

Vandergrift went to the University of North Carolina at Charlotte. The library had an extensive collection of trading and investment books, and he spent all four years reading as much as he could find about how to win in the markets. Most of what he read was trash, but he took the stance that every book had some beneficial nugget, some useful morsel, no matter how small.

He quickly noticed that most books had a trading method or system, even books written in the 1950s. All had a technique you could apply and use to trade. During college he bought SuperCharts—which was the precursor to TradeStation. TradeStation gives you the ability to program trend following rules and test out system ideas. If you have a trading system, idea, or method you want to test and see how it might perform, TradeStation can graphically show you the results. You want to enter on a 100-day breakout and exit on a 100-day breakout, and test it over a diverse number of markets, and boom, you can see the results quickly. This kind of experimentation builds confidence before you ever risk real money.

This was the beginning of Vandergrift developing his own trend following trading system, but that was not yet going to pay his bills. A job was going to be needed following college.

His resume? That was not working too well. Sending resumes out was not enough to get a job then, nor is it today. His cold calling started.

Vandergrift had a process that every month he would try to interview a successful broker in town, thinking that would be his calling. One cold call led him to the only commodity guy in town.

Vandergrift wanted to sit down over lunch. The commodity pro said no to lunch, but he did offer, "If you really want to get your feet wet and you want to get into commodity futures, you need to go see this old man up in the mountains in Hendersonville, North Carolina."

He continued, "Go see John Hill at Futures Truth Company." Vandergrift picked up the phone and called.

Let me stop for a second. What would you have done? Call immediately? Delay? Procrastinate? Make excuses? Go apply for a job at Burger King instead?

Vandergrift graduated on a Saturday and went to work on Monday. He was ready to go and ready to learn the ways of trading.

John Hill's firm called Futures Truth, which is where I first met Vandergrift, purports to independently rank and evaluate trading systems. This was a dream job for Vandergrift. He was able to see trading systems that worked and ones that didn't. Many systems, and you will find this too, fail for a prime reason, namely a lack of risk control. The ones that performed well did so because of universal trading rules (again, trade all markets the same way) and risk control (again, don't bet the farm on every trade).

You are going to find in your education that there are some universal schools of trend following trading: high/low breakouts, single moving average crossovers, multiple moving average crossovers, and Bollinger Band breakouts.

I have talked about breakouts in trend trading already, but let me address other basic trend following systems.

- *Moving average:* An indicator that shows the average value of a security's price over a time period. They are used to emphasize the *trend* and smooth out price fluctuations. A trading system using two moving averages would give a buy signal when the shorter (faster) moving average advances above the longer (slower) moving average. A sell signal would be given when the shorter moving average crosses below the longer moving average. The speed of the systems and the number of signals generated will depend on the length of the moving averages.*

  For example, to calculate a 50-day simple moving average (SMA), add the last 50 closing price values and divide the sum by 50. There are other,

---

*"Arthur Hill on Moving Average Crossovers." See: http://stockcharts.com/help/doku.php?id=chart_school:trading_strategies:arthur_hill_on_movin.

more complex ways to calculate a moving average, but the simple moving average is still the most commonly used. Typical values are 20 and 50 days, although 50 and 200 days are also frequently used.*

- *Bollinger Bands*: A technical analysis tool invented by John Bollinger. They consist of a set of three curves drawn in relation to market prices. The middle band is a measure of the intermediate-term trend, usually a simple moving average, and that serves as the base for the upper band and lower band. The interval between the upper and lower bands and the middle band is determined by volatility, typically the standard deviation of the same data that were used for the average. The default parameters, 20 periods and two standard deviations, may be adjusted.

There are differences in various trend following entry and exit techniques; however, most entries and exits, regardless of precise entry/exit, occur at very similar times. Don't get too excited about when to enter. While entry and exit is an overwhelming focus for new traders, it is only a small part of the recipe for winning in the trend follower's cookbook.

What is much more important? Money management is far more imperative to your success than worrying

*See: http://eresearch.fidelity.com/backtesting/viewstrategy?category= Trend%20Following&wealthScriptType=MovingAverageCrossover.

about a perfect entry. Why? We all have limited money! So what is the right amount to trade on each trade? That brings the risk theme seen across other chapters back into the equation. Risk creates the profits. If there were no risk, then there would be no incentive to trade. More simply, trading wouldn't pay if it were easy. That means controlling risk has to be your obsession.

Early lessons in place, Vandergrift did not last long at Futures Truth. The entrepreneurial bug bit him.

## Putting a System in Place

Introducing a system component into trading is the only way for you to reach the discipline needed to possibly make the big money. Most retail investors blow up, or have a short lived trading career because they don't have the discipline to stick with their system. They are always looking for the quick buck, or the quick fix.

Sadly, every year millions of accounts literally collapse from basic mistakes. What is the most common mistake? You put a trade on, it starts losing money, but your gut tells you to hang on because it's going to work out and go your way. You end up holding on too long to a losing trade. But it has to come back up? No, it doesn't.

A trading system takes that emotion out. It takes the wishing and wanting out of the equation. This type of thinking appeals to everyone once they understand it. Just let the system do what it needs to do, and everything will work its way out in the end. That is the *success* process.

Vandergrift, like many of the trend following traders, found through intense research that the only systems that really worked over time were long term trend following in nature.

However, his real Aha! moment came when he put money management into his trading system equation.

When most people tell you that they are a trend follower, all they are doing is looking at a 100-day moving average or a Bollinger Band system—just like the ones I mentioned. But that's it. They have no money management plan.

Let me give an example to put this in context and better explain the importance of money management. There was a local group of traders near Vandergrift in North Carolina. They had established a money management firm. At one point, they received a "Trader of the Year" award in *Futures Magazine*, a major trading publication.

Vandergrift was friendly with them and watched their trading. He could see that they traded one futures contract for 10-year Treasury notes and one contract for euro dollars. He wondered, "You have to be kidding me. Why would you do that? Just on a margin level 10-year notes are three times that of euro dollars. Why wouldn't you have three euro dollars for every one 10-year note?"

What would you do? Would you try to figure out the discrepancy? How would you go about it? Vandergrift picked up the phone and called to ask why they treated all markets the same when it came to measuring risk.

They quickly cut the conversation off and said, "This is what we do. We are not entertaining questions. This is it."

This was a problem waiting to happen. Vandergrift soon watched their trading program implode. He knew that risk management centered on trading markets equally, from a risk perspective, was mission critical. You just can't favor one market over another. That's what this group did and their program failed. Watching someone go broke in real time was quite educational.

The experience from watching someone implode, in a sense, delayed Vandergrift's trend trading progress. Had that firm not gone through the pain they did, he would not have put so much research and faith into money management. It may have taken him going through their same meltdown experience for him to learn their same lesson.

### Follow the Leader

If you have a portfolio of markets, and you receive a trend following signal to enter, you want to risk an equal amount on every trade. This is foundational to your success. Ignore this wisdom and going broke is the likely alternative.

Think about this trading example. You hypothetically start trading two markets. In the first market, risk is defined as $1,000. On the second market your risk is defined as $250. In order to manage these trades and keep everything equal, you will trade one futures contract of the first market and four contracts of the second market. You're not favoring either one of these markets. This becomes critical, especially in the futures market, when you start trading markets like grains and currencies together. A grain contract, most of the time, is smaller, meaning it controls less capital than that of most currency markets. If you don't trade more contracts of corn to compensate for the larger contract sizes of currencies, you are going to end up favoring currencies over the grain contracts from a risk standpoint.

## Big Picture Philosophical Points

What are your goals? What do you want? How much do you want to make?

Vandergrift was stark: "If I die tomorrow are people going to remember me because my standard deviation of average annual return was XYZ in relation to my compound of average annual growth rate? No. They will

---

**What is your motivation for trading? Are you trading for any other reason than to make big money? If so, stop trading.**

---

remember me because of the wealth that my trading created. That is the whole motivation for me. My trading is not for some arcane statistical measure that no one really understands. I want to make people money and change their lives."

For you to reach that level of confidence and that level of contentment, it is critical for you to learn from other traders.

I learned a tremendous amount from trend following trader Bill Dunn. Vandergrift had a similar learning experience, too, from Dunn. He learned more from watching Bill Dunn's track record, his month-by-month performance numbers (see www.dunncapital.com) versus reading every article in *Futures Magazine* or any of the well known technical trading journals.

The conviction Bill Dunn has had for his trend following trading system and his ability to stick with it since the early 1970s is proof of what can happen when you go for the home run. Yet Dunn is not in it to hit only a home run, rather he is out to hit grand slams. That is what he does, and he has done it exceptionally well and consistently for decades.

Accepting Vandergrift's belief and accepting Dunn's track record is not easy. There are so many distractions that can knock you away from the real goal. Look at CNBC programs on air every day. They talk about the greatest stock now, the greatest this, the greatest that, whatever the distraction may be, but none of them regularly brings up the fact that the NASDAQ is in a 10-year drawdown. No one wants to report that the S&P has returned nearly zero growth from buying and holding mutual funds over the last decade.

Trend following is not *that*. It is not average. It is above average.

Vandergrift talked about average. He was talking with a doctor, a very successful doctor. The doctor kept talking about index investing and the S&P 500. Vandergrift stopped him short:

"When you went to medical school did you ever want to graduate with a C average?" The doctor said, "No." Vandergrift replied, "Do you want to send your kids to a C school?" He said, "No." Vandergrift countered, "Then why are you doing that with your money? The S&P is an average. It's an average of the 500 largest companies in the United States. It's an average. It's a C index. Why would you want to invest to get average returns?"

That is one of the most important questions any would-be trend following trader must ask, but it does not stop there.

## Piling On

Above average returns really start with compounding.

You want to know the difference between being rich and poor in the United States, or in life for that matter? Three percentage points—that's it. If you take a 12 percent annual return compounded monthly, over the course of 30 years, basically the working career of the average person, every dollar that you invested will be worth $35.94.

If you compound a 15 percent annual return compounded monthly over 30 years, can you take a guess of the return difference? Is it 10 percent better or 50 percent? No. Every dollar invested would be worth $87.54 a difference of 143 percent over 12 percent.

It is only three percentage points, but compounded over 30 years that makes a tremendous difference. That is why you have to shoot for the higher return. Even if it is two percentage points more—it is a huge difference.

Chapter Nine

# You Can't Know
# Everything

*Eric Crittenden and Cole Wilcox*

THE ESSENCE OF AGNOSTICISM IS NOT KNOWING ONE WAY or the other, and not attempting to put a firm belief onto what you do not know. These days I am so used to the concept of making money in up markets and down markets, regardless of the market, that I sometimes forget how foreign that concept is for the average trader or investor. It's like a rollercoaster, up and down, up and down, up, up, down, down—with no predictable pattern as to when up will happen or down will happen. The idea is to wait and let the market move in a direction–either way–and then follow it. Eric Crittenden and Cole Wilcox exemplify this critical principle in their trend following trading.

Over the years, many hedge funds, commodity trading advisors, proprietary traders, and global macro funds have successfully applied trend following methods to profitably trade in global futures markets. Very little research, however, has been published regarding trend following strategies as applied to individual stocks (even though 100 years ago trend following started on stocks). Oh sure, many trade stock indexes that have been around for decades, but there has been less focus on trend trading individual stocks.

Crittenden and Wilcox noticed there were no public firms applying trend following to individual stocks and they could not figure out why. It didn't make any sense, since that's where much of the money in the world was going.

They developed a trend following approach for stocks. Their basic plan was to buy breakout stocks and use a trailing stop as they advanced. To do this effectively you have to be wired to understand the relationship between risk and reward, an understanding that skews the odds in your favor.

You want to view yourself as a professional speculator—regardless of silly attacks on speculators coming from the President and the press. Speculation is our lifeblood. It is a necessity since it helps to set the price in a free market. Without it, we are nowhere.

And as a speculator, price action, or movement, is what matters because it is the only thing that shows up on your account statement. Faith in something else less specific such as buy and hold, index investing, and so on is a highly addictive and incredibly expensive drug. Successful investors and speculators should have a very skeptical and visceral reaction to group handholding. It's just not where you want to be for long-term success.

## Follow the Leader

Trend following works on stocks, too, and who better to teach us than two guys who wrote a paper called, "Does Trend Following Work on Stocks?" It outlined their strategy. They use a 10 ATR stop. ATR stands for "average true range." The true range is simply how far a stock moves in a given day, like standard deviation, but it includes the gaps— if a stock gaps up or gaps down. So for General Electric (NYSE: GE), its average true range might be $0.80 right now. That is the typical daily move, including the gap. So they multiply the ATR by 10 and trail that from the purchase price, which is the all-time high. Their stops on average are about

*(Continued)*

28 to 30 percent away for a typical stock. For a really volatile stock, it might be 50 percent away. For a really quiet stock, it might be as close as 10 or 12 percent. The average true range measures the volatility of the stock in question, so your trailing stop loss is adjusted according to each stock's volatility. That type of thinking, a counterintuitive system—that's what you want.

## Starting Out

Wilcox started with zero money. He came from a family without great wealth, so he had to focus on survival from the beginning. Nobody was going to be there with a checkbook to back him.

In his first job as a broker he had one shot at making it, and surviving. He knew the stark truth deep in his gut that nobody was going to recapitalize him if he failed. He knew that he had to make his clients money. Making a 100 percent effort at all times did not allow much time for relaxation. He was a 19-year-old kid at the time, not knowing anything except that he couldn't waste time and couldn't afford a catastrophic loss.

There was a developing philosophy too. Perhaps it is one you can relate to: Wilcox never accepted what others told him. He always asked questions to get to the truth regardless of consequences—even as a child.

Crittenden's first job out of college was teaching. He taught business math, database programming, and spreadsheet programming in high school.

However, he quickly shifted gears. One of the wealthier families in Kansas had their family office in Wichita. Crittenden was offered a job that paid a lot more. No more teaching!

This family was no slouch. They started with about $250 million in 1996 and bankrolled that to close to $900 million at the time he started working there—which was the height of the dot-com bubble.

However, there was a not so rosy undercurrent. Sometimes, for some people, once they have made a certain amount of money, they begin to take to trading differently. Crittenden was comfortable looking at the disaster scenarios, trying to assess their probability. He was blunt, "These people were not really interested in managing their risk."

He tried to explain scenarios by which they could lose money in short order. They didn't want to hear any of what he had to say. They wanted Crittenden to be a happy cheerleader, not a risk manager.

Eventually markets started to go down in 2000 and this wealthy family started increasing their leverage. They were trying to make their money back on losses, and fast.

However, they didn't sell losing positions. They actually started selling winning positions in order to free up capital to recapitalize the losing positions. Crittenden saw the unfolding disaster: "No, you can't do that. That's how you go to zero."

The personalities in this wealthy family changed. They became different people. They were of a certain manner on the ride up, kindhearted, decent people, and they lost their way to some degree on the ride down. It affected their psychology. It became all about making the money back, but they didn't make it back.

Watching that round-trip disaster affected Crittenden dramatically.

He became so disengaged that he wrote a letter to the family voicing his disagreement with their overly aggressive risk appetite. If he was concerned with politics and protecting his job, the letter—a version of "take this job and shove it"—was not a wise career move.

However, jobs were not Crittenden's or Wilcox's calling. It was entrepreneur time—or it would be once they met. As Crittenden finished working for the Kansas-based family, he decided *Going to California* was the song to play. It was time for a fresh start. On the way there he was passing through Arizona to see his mother. He liked the state and decided to stay. He floated resumes around, and in a classic small world story, one made it across Wilcox's brokerage desk.

Crittenden recalled seeing Wilcox at his office for the first time. His shirt was untucked and he had a headset strapped on. He looked like he'd been in a 12-round fight with George Foreman or someone who just needed water. Crittenden thought to himself, "This is your typical day?" It was not something he wanted anything to do with.

But they hit it off and decided to do a project to either prove or disprove classic Wall Street theories and axioms that had been passed down from mentor types. The big question: what worked and what didn't work in trading?

None of the trading ideas they tested worked. Nothing was consistently effective.

Well, if you don't have anything that works, who does? That was their next question. When they started looking around at trading winners, the first trader that they became interested in, and wanted to learn more about, was trend following trader Salem Abraham.

In early 2002 they met Abraham and were exposed to the world of trend following (You can read more about Salem Abraham in my book, *The Complete Turtle Trader*). They spent a great deal of time reading through his regulatory *disclosure documents* (one of the insights I had learned early on too), reading articles about him, and trying to understand what it was that he was doing to make so much money.

They continued to consume as much research as possible about the systematic methods behind the many trend following pioneers—including several of the trend traders in earlier chapters of this book. Surprisingly, they said my web site, TurtleTrader.com, was also an invaluable research tool in their process.

They subscribed to multiple databases that reported individual pro trend following traders' performance and began to perform quantitative and qualitative evaluations of those traders. Not unlike the journey I took, they set out to talk to as many great trend following traders as possible. They flew all over the world, on their dime, to further their education (And for those who think today that only sending a letter or an e-mail is enough to gain an audience with trading legends—wise up.)

What they found was that most traditional trend following traders had never even looked at individual stocks—they generally traded stock indexes on futures markets. This was the pivot point to the start of a multi-year research project to determine the viability of using systematic trend following on stocks.

---

**The most traditional trend following traders
never even look at individual stocks.**

What does their research have to you with your trading? It's their process. Their process is how you need to approach it too. They were never hung up on being *right*; rather they were interested in not staying *wrong*. Wilcox, for example, has a constant process of asking, "Am I wrong?" while he sees everyone else asking, "Am I right?" If you don't ask the correct probing question with genuine curiosity, like a scientist, you cannot arrive at the correct answer. Right?

Anything successful in life is a process of trial and error. You try something, you look at the results, and you eliminate what doesn't work. The scientific method doesn't allow you to prove anything. All you can do is disprove theories, and then, with a preponderance of evidence still left, you can accept and keep the remainder as long as you can't disprove it. Wouldn't it be nice to see Joe Kernen come on CNBC and say that some day?

### Follow the Leader

Lumpy returns are good for you. Write that down.

In this "business," most people fail. Even most professional money managers fail to outperform the market, so if you find yourself doing what makes

(*Continued*)

most people comfortable, then you have to accept the results that most people get, and that is failure. You want to do something counterintuitive. What Crittenden and Wilcox found is that the small minority of stocks that generate all of the market's returns have only one thing in common: a propensity to keep hitting new all-time highs for a long time.

So, mathematically speaking, you absolutely have to do the opposite of what the majority does, otherwise you simply can't get ahead; it is not possible. Most people automatically gravitate toward high winning percentages. They want low drawdown, low volatility; they want all these things because those are symptoms of health—or at least they think those equal health. Unfortunately, they are more concerned with the symptoms than they are of the outcome. And most of those people are paying a premium to enjoy those things that they think signify health. You have to be doing the opposite, and that is high-payoff, low-winning-percentage trades, or said another way—lumpy returns. That is what works.

Not having any margin of safety led Crittenden and Wilcox to seek out an assortment of mentors—to try and ensure their success. Tom Basso, a very successful trend trader in the Phoenix area at the time, provided seed capital. He was a partner with their original firm from the beginning. Some readers may recall Basso's profile from Jack Schwager's classic book, *The New Market Wizards*.

Basso liked their thinking, and pointed them in the right directions. He would say, "Talk to these people, they are good. Avoid those people over there." That might sound simple, but when someone with decades of experience points you in the right direction, you have to be in a position to understand why that type of wisdom is different. Do you just trust and not verify? Of course not, but traders, especially ones who have done well for years, are going to save you tremendous time on your trading journey. Why is Joe Torre's expertise invaluable as a baseball manager? He has been there. He has done it. Oh, sure you can go figure it out on your own from scratch, but why not take a shortcut on the learning curve? That happens to be the reason that this book has come together as it has—to get you there faster.

## Trim the Fat

A few key lessons from Basso helped Crittenden and Wilcox from the beginning. Basso was blunt, "It really is simple. You hold your winners, have discipline and cut your losers. You take what the market gives and you'll be successful in this business."

Crittenden added: "One. Don't over-bet. Two. Diversify across markets. You might see a guy who has a great track record and he trades long only the S&Ps. They don't last very long."

If you bring a person off the street, give him a bunch of money with no instruction, and tell him to start trading, he will sell his winners, and double up on his losers. He'll try to get a high winning percentage. His losers will be bigger than his winners. After a certain period of time his account equity will hit zero.

You don't learn the right way at college either. "You go to a university and there are big buildings. It's got departments, professors, and all sorts of people that work there. We had to create our own trend trading university," said Wilcox.

There's no class or university that teaches you how to be a successful speculator. None. They don't exist. There is nothing available. They're teaching something else in schools, and whatever it is, it's not how to be a successful speculator or how to take money and make positive returns.

Let's face it, schools teach you how to fit into the existing system. You need to ask the big question, "What is the correct system for me?" Most just accept the status quo, get their degree, and fit inside the box doing whatever they are told to do. At the end of a career, with that backwards thinking, you clean out your cube and go home. After all, *The Office* has been wildly popular because it is all too real.

Crittenden and Wilcox always take the approach of looking at the system and asking, "Is it right or is it wrong?" Most people don't do this. When a teacher is lecturing and a student raises his hand to point out a contradiction, generally the teacher tells the student to pipe down and learn the material as written. Many teachers don't discuss or theorize. They pontificate. They are, after all, cogs in a system—a system that doesn't lend itself much to heretics.

## You Have to Know Your Strategy

Wilcox put forward the counterintuitive notion when addressing the super-hyped investment of the day—gold. "Technically, buying gold is a strategy. It's not just a trading instrument. If you listen to TV commercials on gold they will tell you to buy gold. You buy it, and you've just undertaken *some* strategy. Now, understand that strategy doesn't necessarily have an exit point, which is no small issue. Many hear buy gold, and they're assuming that there's a strategy built in to protect on the downside. Just buying gold should actually lead you to think, then what?"

Unfortunately, the way humans make decisions is to focus on returns alone. They never focus on the risk component of what they are doing.

For example, without understanding the sell component when you buy something like gold, you can't understand the risk component because you have not defined it. If I say I'm going to buy at X price and sell it at Y price and I'm going to allocate X dollars to it, well, I can determine that X dollars, this-minus-this is going to lead to this amount of loss if it goes down and bites me. You can box the risk in and you can understand it. However, just buying gold, with no exit in place, doesn't box anything in. Is there a lot of swimming naked in gold markets today? You bet.

You want to make a point of never focusing daily on the return component of your trading. Good trend following will keep you in that frame of mind at all times. You don't make a decision to allocate capital or make an investment without knowing your exit strategy first.

You can only control where you get out of a position once you put it on. You cannot control what's going to happen. You can only control how you react.

No one controls future events. None of your analysis is going to be able to control a future event. Why focus your time and energy trying to predict an outcome that you have no control of? No one else knows either, so don't worry that the suits on TV know something you don't.

Further, taking too much risk because you get paid more in the short term is a recipe for long-term disaster. If you are overdoing your risk, it will come back to take your money and send you back to the poorhouse. The short term, however, may be a decade, you just don't know. It might be one week, but regardless of the time component, you don't want to be in a position to lose all of your money after one year, five years, or ten years of work. Or do you?

Bottom line, you are up against the natural bias in the way human beings make decisions, which is to reward outcomes. If a guy is an A student, he's obviously smart, right? At least that is the assumption. If a money manager has a good track record and a five-star fund rating, he's good, right? Not necessarily. How could you possibly know if he's good or not? You have to evaluate the process by how that outcome was generated. If you don't do that, you have nothing and know nothing.

Sear that thought into your trend following memory bank.

## Chapter Ten

# Make It Work Across All Markets

*Michael Clarke*

MOST PEOPLE FIRST PONDER TRADING AND THINK, "HOW could I ever trade soybeans, gold, wheat, Apple, Japanese yen, and Swiss francs successfully?" Those markets, to the beginner's eye, seemingly have nothing in common. But if you take a step back and analyze the price data, you can see that they do, in fact, have an important common denominator.

Blur your eyes and imagine a chart, a price chart, hanging on the wall. Now imagine you don't know the name of the chart. It's just a chart. Don't they all look the same if you take the name away? Is there really a difference? So do you really care about the economics behind oil? Or do you just want to make money from a trend delivering, for example, a 25 percent return? What if the 25 percent return came from soybeans or the Brazilian *real*—why do you care where your 25 percent return came from?

That's why you want to know Michael Clarke and his wisdom.

Clarke has traded hundreds of millions of dollars for clients over nearly 20 years. He has traded client money to produce profit margins that no investor would complain about. What is a great example of his success in action? He started shorting crude oil in the summer of 2008 when it hovered around $140. He stayed with that trade down, going short, to $80 before getting out—collecting the bulk of the downtrend. Was he an expert in oil? No, and neither were any of the other trend followers trading oil. Were they experts in OPEC policy or whether or not tensions were flaring in the Middle East? Nope. No expertise in any of that.

Clarke didn't start out as a trend following trader.

When Clarke first began programming while attending college in 1967, he was already thinking in terms of numbers, "I wanted to list all the possible combinations of numbers one through five, and so I wrote a little program to do that." He wrote a program with a little loop, inside a loop, inside a loop, and figured out that loops inside each other were the basis of programming success. Clarke had his Aha! moment.

He thought, "Geez! This is really cool! It's really fun and challenging. It makes you think." This realization hooked Clarke into the *game* of programming—a precursor thought process that would come in handy in trading arenas soon enough.

Not surprisingly, his first career was as a software developer. He says, "I loved the challenge of developing integrated software solutions for different kinds of businesses, especially manufacturers. It's a complex process to provide systems to handle functions like acquiring raw materials, putting them together, selling them, and collecting the funds for those sales. One needs to be adept at both the overall concept of how everything fits together as well as the details of implementation."*

As we all try to do at one time or another, Clarke tried the corporate grind. There was a programming competition during college and he won first place. The prize was consideration for a job working for Procter & Gamble in

*"Clarke Capital Management," The Barclay Group, 4th quarter, 1999.

Cincinnati—no small deal to those familiar with P&G and its legacy in Cincinnati. He only had to get through the perfunctory interview. His foot was already in the door, but at the time he was a little "wild"—that would equate to a motorcycle and long hair.

He went to the interview and didn't exactly dress up. Procter & Gamble is very "white shirt and tie." Clarke had his interview, but they wanted nothing to do with him. He heard back, "Nobody's going to like you looking like that."

Time to try something else.

## No More Suit and Tie

Wall Street soon called, as that was where the real money was. However, Clarke was not a great salesperson and the 1987 stock crash, followed by the mini-crash in 1989, left him searching.

He had to find something new, and fast.

One problem: He could not convince anyone that he knew what he was doing.

He began looking into trading systems. He originally bought the System Writer Plus package to test technical buying and selling ideas (a precursor to TradeStation) and found it inadequate for what he wanted to do. Consequently, Clarke bit the bullet and developed his own system-testing platform. He developed the ability to test his mechanical trading system ideas from scratch!

Clarke had read many books on trading, but the first book he found that went into the details of trend trading systems was Bruce Babcock's *The Business One Irwin Guide to Trading Systems*. It was instrumental in his initial trading. Babcock described a system that went across the board making money in all markets. It was a great robust system that could be quantified and systematized. And it worked. That revelation hit Clarke in the solar plexus— the idea that a book had a way to apply some simple rules and make money. "Wow!" he thought.

## What's the Magic Sauce?

Why do trend following systems work? There is no great answer, and Clarke would concur. All he knows is that trend following trading systems have worked for a very long time.

But many don't get that. They say, "What's copper doing?" "What do you think copper is going to do tomorrow?" "Is copper in a bull market?" "Do you know what's happening?" People want a story.

Trend followers don't have a clue, and Clarke is no different. That said, he will tell skeptics an opinion if they want one. But it all goes back to the fact that the models *succeed*. He stands by his trend following models, "There is no sense in taking a 50/50 shot in predicting anything. Just follow the models."

"Here are my opinions *but* . . ." Those opinions just don't substitute for trading system models.

## Using a System

If Clarke's trend trading model says "sell this market," he sells. He doesn't argue with his trading system.

---
$\sim$

**Never, ever argue with your trading system.**

---

Everything Clarke does is programmed into his software. Of course, there is plenty of work that goes into the research and building of a trend trading system that you are comfortable with, but after it is built, and your rules are programmed in, you just follow what it says. This is not fundamental (no crop reports, no Fed watches, no OPEC news, no unemployment reports) at all. You could program fundamentals into a model, but that is not the road Clarke has taken. It's not the road you want to be driving down either.

After Clarke built something that worked for him, he said to himself, "This is a pretty good system. I can compete with the professionals."

This is the short and sweet version of how Clarke became a professional trend trader. It's not sexy or entertaining, but his story has built an empire of money.

To this day, the sole reason he is still in the trading game is for the joy he extracts from it. Don't underestimate passion in the success equation. How does success translate for him? For one, he has always worked out of his suburban home in Hinsdale, Illinois, about 25 miles from downtown Chicago. Can you be anywhere and trade? Yes, you can. Does that mean Indonesia? Yes. Singapore? Yes. Anywhere? Yes.

What system lessons can you take from Clarke that can help your account grow?

You want to look for trend following models that remain robust over long time periods and you want to be willing to include models that have flat to negative performance for periods of up to two years. The principles that allow a good model to work successfully may fall out of favor and stop working for a period of time, but if the model has validity, the long-term principles will reassert themselves over time. Don't jump the gun in throwing away your models. Clarke emphasizes, "We don't want to throw an otherwise excellent model away simply because it had one or two rough stretches. If it meets our overall criteria and blends well with other models, we'll use it."*

You can go through long periods of no movement in the markets with trend following strategies and then all of a sudden, boom! You will get a huge run-up, as markets all start

*"Clarke Capital Management," The Barclay Group, 4th quarter, 1999.

trending at the same time. It's like being in the desert for 11 months with no rain. All of the sudden it begins pouring and flowers grow. You are happy and flying high again.

---

**There is no secret. You can describe this way of being, this way of trading, in one word—patience.**

---

In the 25 years Clarke has been trading he has gone through the emotional rollercoasters. He has thought that his trading career was toast on many occasions. He would say to himself, "Now, this is it. We're never going to make money again. I've been lucky for 25 years, and now it's perhaps soon over!"

How do you deal with the ups and downs? Strict trading rules are the only magic salve to possibly save you from the dreaded emotional mistakes that can blow up your account.

These days, Clarke doesn't worry about his trend model. He knows his systems will pull through. He doesn't sleep well at night in general, but it's not because of trading. The no-sleep worrying from the stress of trading ended for him well over a decade ago.

## Follow the Leader

Clarke is all about going back in time to test a trading model. You want to have a sound philosophy when developing your trading model and test it using a large pool of markets. Clarke used approximately 105 markets, with data as far back as 1945. In order for a model to be accepted, you want it to trade all markets using the same rules and parameters. Your results should yield good performance across 90-plus percent of all markets tested. Also, no model should be accepted unless it shows stability of performance during tests involved with shifting parameters and altering rules. This is the definition of robust.

*Source:* www.clarkecap.com.

While it's common knowledge today to those who already understand or trade trend following methods, Clarke didn't trade European or any foreign markets when he started. He traded only domestic U.S. markets, as he had only developed his trend trading models on those markets.

One day he decided to add foreign markets. He put them into his system and they worked fine. No tweaking was necessary. He saw for the first time the eye opening universality with his trend trading models. It was yet another Aha! moment.

However, building a trading approach that is flexible can be debated.

I once sat down with a bright trader. She told me, "I just met with [name] trend follower, who you know is very successful. All they kept telling me was how much they're tweaking their models and constantly improving them."

My response, "I don't believe it. They tell *stories* for people who don't understand trend following. That's the story they're creating to make you feel comfortable."

Clarke agreed, "You're exactly right. You can almost pick up on what some people want to hear. Do they want to hear that you tweak the models or do they want to hear that you have them? Some people want to hear that you're constantly adjusting to the market. But the fact of the matter is that there is no constant tweaking. The markets are ever evolving, but certain criteria are forever constant. Changing markets is what we make money off of. It's human nature in a way for some people. If you don't really have *their* story, they can't relate. You basically give them the answer you think they want to hear. It's like the poker players, they can look at you and figure out what you want to hear."

People ask, "Well, how are you keeping track with the changes in the markets?" Clarke was clear. "It's dynamically built in. Our models are all adaptive and dynamic."

If you've done your trend trading homework properly, you don't have to adapt your trend following nonstop to whatever is perceived as *world change*.

## Fundamental Folly

I was once at a hedge fund conference with MBA students and allocators (people who give institutional money to firms like Clarke's). One of the prominent speakers, one with a hedge fund, asked rhetorically, "How many of you think rates will be higher or lower in the next period?"

Having received my MBA too, and having learned nothing during that time about trend following trading, the speaker's question immediately bored me. I started to think, "Well, I assume he has some skill from the fundamental side that allows him to decide when to buy and sell . . ." However, he went through his presentation with assorted economic indicators, and there was no *there, there*. I felt like I was back in a graduate level economics class, wondering whether there was a connection between these ratios and statistics to actually making money.

I could not connect the dots. I didn't know how, after listening to his presentation, this man bought or sold anything. I just knew that he had outlined his fundamental predictions. He was obviously a bright man, or I thought he was.

Clarke saw it, "They know how to leverage [and go "long"] and they know how to borrow cheap and [trade] at six to one leverage [and that's it]."

The leveraged long strategies Clarke refers to work for a while, until they bust out like clockwork. They are the root of every big name blowup over the last 20 years.

## Stories Don't Make You Money

These days, millions are watching CNBC and any number of other "make you money get out of debt" shows. In the old days, it was one pragmatic show: *Wall $treet Week*. Today, the new money shows are a circus. Further, there are brokers and fundamental research everywhere now, all promising you tomorrow's headlines today. The pushing of fundamentally driven stories at a breakneck pace is the new normal. And the demand is there. People want to understand so badly, and stories help to rationalize. It's comfort food for the financial soul.

For example, many buy stocks that they *use*. You go to Wal-Mart, where you buy toilet paper and sponges. Wal-Mart is tangible for you. You see the store congested with people, so you think it must be making large profits. So you buy stock in Wal-Mart, assuming the stock can only go up, based on your observations. It seems logical to conclude. Or if you're going to Starbucks for vanilla lattes and you like them and you see other people there taking coffee shots, then why not buy Starbucks stock? People operate with that mentality.

The idea that you're doing something mathematical (like trend following) and that it can work is not digestible for many. Most people do not understand statistics and probabilities, and don't want to. It's too cold, and it doesn't allow them to talk up a fun story at the next dinner party. Try telling someone, "I'm doing this mathematically and grinding it out with a bunch of small losses because I really have no idea what the market will do next." No one finds that exciting!

People want to be able to tell their buddy at the gym, the guy on the golf course, their wife, their girlfriend, or anyone with a pulse—the story: "I knew Starbucks was going to be big before it ever was."

Clarke, on the other hand, turns on his computer and pushes a button every morning that shoots his trades out for the day, at least if there are any for that day. He sits there and watches. Some times when he loses he puts his helmet on, goes to his desk, and sits there for a few months until his trend trading system wins again. It is a never-ending cycle, but a damn profitable one.

## Motivation and Drive

Who likes saying "yes sir!" to a hovering boss every day? Like most entrepreneurs, Clarke didn't exactly mesh well working for the man. He never had a boss he liked.

In fact, he sees much of his success today, and the career choices he has made, as attributable to being a loner. If he were better looking, or more popular, he is quite certain he would have chosen another life route.

"Gee, if I had another life I would come back really handsome, well-built, an athlete, attract a lot of girls . . ."

But if it comes down to being less on the intellectual side, the choice isn't easy for him. He isn't saying he would want the same upbringing he had, but having some bad things in your childhood can develop motivational fuel. That kind of motivation can be a very effective driver to success.

Can you relate to that? It is that kind of thinking that set Clarke's drive and determination on course to be a winning trend following trader.

When Clarke was initially establishing his trend trading routine, he would work long hours and love it. He would get up at 3 A.M. with ideas flowing. I did the same thing with my business. I was often so naturally wired that I could not sleep. I was ready to get to the next day already.

If Clarke were handsome and popular rather than a loner, would he have had the time to focus, to think, and to translate over and over trend trading processes in his head? Would he have had the time to search for a workable trading methodology? Who knows! Everyone is different. Everyone has different drives.

However, you have to have *it* in your gut to win. If you don't have *it* or if you won't work to get *it*, go hang out at the bar and commiserate with the other patrons who all imagine themselves one step away from success—of course only after they down just one more whiskey shot.

## Sheep Need Not Apply

People in markets always move in a sheep-like mass. They move like lemmings. That will never change. Maybe the devices used, and their views, will change, but people are people. So if you want to make it, if you want to pull something off that is different, you've got to think outside the box. You've got to look at things with a critical eye. You've got to say, "What's different?" "What can I do?" "How can I figure this out?"

Having various combinations of skills has been essential to Clarke's success. The ability to program his own systems was top in his mind. Giving his ideas to someone else to program would never have worked for him. He had to actually do it himself. That was his confidence. Does every trend follower do it that way? No, but Clarke did.

You've got to come at trend trading from a different angle, not just an average angle, and it ultimately traces back to an entrepreneurial mindset. I recently told friends that the best trading book I had read in years had nothing to do with trading: *Linchpin*, by Seth Godin.

Michael Clarke lived Godin's book long before it was written.

# Chapter Eleven

# Stay in the Moment of Right Now

*Charles Faulkner*

PERHAPS YOU HAVE HEARD THE EXPRESSION ABOUT LIVING in the moment of *now*. What do I mean? The past is gone and the future is unknowable, but we have right now. That does not mean we cannot consider our past experiences or mistakes as useful references. Nor does that mean we cannot prepare and plan for the future. It does mean that making decisions based upon what is actually happening in the moment of right now is how great trend following traders organize their lives and produce their fortunes.

While not primarily a trader, Charles Faulkner brings a tremendously useful insight to the table. In all my years I can think of no one who does a better job of bringing traders and investors to a better understanding of themselves. Understanding yourself as a trader is the needed introduction to the journey of success in trend following profits.

Faulkner sees the world from a very wide and novel perspective, and you should too.

Case in point: A crucial lesson to understand is that when entering the market game, losses are part of the game. No matter the amount of experience you have, there will always be losses. That said, you want to make sure your losses are ones that you can handle—knowing that they are emotionally going to affect you.

People in sports understand this. Professional game players understand that to build your skill, you need to take losses and learn from them. You hope to play against people better than you because that is what makes you better.

Studying traders is very useful because everything in their world is extremely focused due to the intensity of their profession. What might take months or years to unfold in an ordinary life can unfold very quickly for traders.

For example, for many people the biggest purchase they make is a house or a car. And for many successful trend traders that kind of money can go through their hands within an hour, or even minutes.

This means, when trading, you don't want to view money in terms of dollars as if you were going to buy a new car, but rather use the dollars to keep score. Putting yourself into that mental framework is critical. Releasing your mind from how you value money in terms of shopping, and instead focusing on it as a score during the game, is a huge first step.

---

**Critically observe how the world works. If you're looking down from 35,000 feet and saying, "Okay, I looked out the window, I know what's going on," you're missing it. You have to think about it critically for yourself.**

---

## Take Advice

We don't like to take advice, but we often do. However, taking advice is putting somebody else in charge. Emotionally, it is taking a one-down position to them. What do they know that you don't?

Financially, it is entrusting your financial wellbeing to somebody else. Intellectually, it is making yourself less stupid and less responsible because you are turning your money over to somebody else.

In a sense, taking advice from someone who knows a field is a completely normal thing. We learn to drive from our parents, a relative, or a driving instructor. We learn sports from coaches who give the wider perspective. They give us the beginnings of our abilities, and then we move on to others who can help take our skills further.

In that sense, taking financial advice makes perfect sense. You know you don't know. And knowing you don't know, you say, "Well, who knows?"

But this is where it gets curious. In the world of professional baseball or other big league sports, you can see a person's performance in black and white. Further, because of the physical reality of it, you see they have talent, and statistical proof, and to go to them is to go to someone who knows their craft.

That same assumption gets applied to financial advice too, but, unfortunately, there is a real chance that the person who made money last season did so by chance. Many of them do not actually have any skills—they were lucky.

This becomes a conundrum. If you don't know, how are you supposed to pick somebody who knows? Most people say, "This person made money last year, I should listen to him." And again, in a non-money world, this would make sense. If somebody was good at cooking or somebody was good at producing films, you'd say, "Well, this person would be a good bet for next year." Wolfgang Puck is a good bet. Spielberg is a good bet, and so on.

This is the challenge. In other words, how do you vet the person who promises to make money? How do you decide if this person is someone you want to take advice from? If it was somebody who knew how to repair cars, you would watch him repair a few cars and say, "I can trust this person's skill."

We look for people who have knowledge of a subject, but the mystery of money, the mystery of finance, is who knows? Who has real knowledge of this? Is it that they can run an actuary table? Or do they have the ability to compound interest? Does that mean they know? This is an especially difficult question given the emotional potency of money, since people tend to look right at the end result. With a game like chess, how you play is very important—the people who truly understand will win more games and for longer—with less fluke-like wins. You would not just take advice from one person who wins a few chess games—you want to learn from someone who understands the process.

When it comes to finding someone who gives financial advice, you want to be looking not only at their results, but how did they get there? Do they have a good process? Does that process allow for mistakes? Does it allow them to get better and better?

That is how you need to psychologically think about winning as a trend following trader.

## Responsibility

Money is responsibility. It is a currency for life. For people who do not want to be responsible with money, it is like saying, "I'm not going to be responsible for my time, and how I use it." That type of person is living in a reactive mode. Merely reacting to stimuli is not charting out a course for a fulfilling life. It is no different from a wild animal responding only to events just to sustain its basic needs (read: fight or flight). That is not a happy or particularly satisfying existence for human beings.

You need to define your edge, a place in your life, where you can be proactive and begin to directly participate in the choices you make, whether it is with your time, your money, or other meaningful things in your life.

That's hard. The whole media cultural milieu now is one where you ought to be gratifying yourself immediately. Very few are discussing, or reflecting, or seemingly thinking about how you can save, invest, or increase your assets in wise or smart ways.

The actual messages in media can run against each other. No wonder it's more difficult now for people to become financially independent. The thinking isn't in society. It used to be the province of rationalism and traditional religion to educate people to take a longer view and make better decisions, but that now falls to financial planners (and worse, to 24/7 financial media).

For example, think about people who watch 17 hours of television a day. You might be one of them! What's shown on television will be your memories. You will not have memories of being with your kids, walking in the woods, sitting in front of a screen and trading correctly, or planning with your spouse for the future.

Digital images from the media—reality TV if you will—will be the only memories you end up with. As sad as it sounds, many decided to join Wall Street after seeing the movie *Wall Street* because they thought Oliver Stone's Gordon Gecko was a good guy. More did it because of Gordon Gecko than Warren Buffett or Jim Rogers or some person of actual achievement. We're tremendously influenced by the potency of media.

Why do we go in these directions? Even if it's anticipating the future, you feel gratified now. In sports one of the issues that separates amateurs from serious professionals is that they feel no gratification from just playing and losing. The gratification for professionals comes when they lose, go back and practice, and then play another day knowing they will win this next time around.

So a big difference that has happened in our society is not only instant gratification, it is also the degree of gratification pushed by media stimulus. It is overpowering for most. People are given repeat messages about what they must want, or they must respond to the latest cell phone advertisement, or the next hybrid car innovation. That is all a business designed to herd the masses to some desired end.

It is sort of like the old story: There is a guy, and he is drinking liquor and smoking cigarettes because early in his life he had seen the ads with the whiskey and the girl and the cigarettes and he's wondering now, "Where are the girls?" as he gets older. You can look at all these different offers being made across the spectrum, and each one of them says that you ought to be gratified *now*, and so consequently people think they ought to be.

Even though some investors may have made a plan, when they see and hear these messages many times a day they can't help but respond to the nonstop offers. Look at Jim Cramer. His show is filled with movement, sound, and all kinds of stimulating input. That messaging captivates many.

Faulkner sees the insanity: "Cramer's show is vivid, immediate, sensory, full of sound, and movement. We're designed to respond to that. We can't help but respond to that. Even though, of course, *Barron's* magazine has pointed out that if you actually followed Cramer's recommendations, you wouldn't be doing very well at all. But people don't seem to mind because they get to feel this closeness with somebody who is active and doing stuff. They see Cramer as intelligent and he seems to know what he is talking about. He is saying these things with a great deal of authority. How can someone with so much vigor be so wrong? My god, he has got to be right!"

You need to develop your capacity to be your own person. You need to be the one who makes decisions based on your circumstances. There needs to be a point at which you can look at TV talking heads and go, "That's just a point of view."

That's the mindset you need as a foundation.

## Human Nature

You don't need to academically research the concept of "hunting and gathering." Anyone who has ever been to a modern grocery store realizes that clever advertisers and marketing strategies crowd the isles together to get us to hunt and gather for our foods. It's well known that Fortune 500 companies now hire anthropologists to try and give us more satisfaction than we actually need as human beings. This is what we are up against.

Efficiency, and who we are as human beings, do not really fit together. We are not designed for efficiency. We are designed to satisfy a tendency to take the best decision that we can, grab hold of it, and enforce it in the present moment. And even if that holds us back later, we do not really mind. In fact, we often try to make a bad process work for as long as possible, that is until it finally breaks and we actually give up, forcing us to try something more promising.

That is quite different from how our modern technologies have developed along a more efficient, automated, and reliable frontier. Whereas we can be distracted by an interesting looking person or by a certain odor—inconsequential random acts that distract us—computers and rigid trading strategies like trend following are not persuaded by emotional stimuli. It is more of a challenge than people realize: How do you stay focused on what really matters?

Think about it. We do not stick with our money decisions just because we made them, but rather, we stick with them because they are *us*. For example, many traders as long as they have not actually sold a losing stock can pretend that it is not a loss. Yet, of course, that is a reality-unreality strategy. A loss is a loss regardless of how you rationalize it.

But it goes deeper than that.

The dog disappears in the morning but is outside the kitchen door by evening. If your kid says he is going to run away, he is back by dinner. And when you lose your car keys (buried on the kitchen table), for some reason they show up a little later on the kitchen table right where you lost them.

As creatures, we're actually designed to think that what we lose is going to come back, and if you think back to most of human history, that was probably true. People didn't often get past the village gate in medieval times.

---

**If a piece of gold or currency is lying on the ground, fundamental traders would say that it can't be real because somebody would have picked it up already.**

---

So the idea of cutting your losses quickly and letting your gains run is in fact going against human biology. That is why so many trend traders are called contrarians. It is not that they are just contrary, although many of them are. It's that they have to be optimistic in a situation where most people would be pessimistic. Trend followers take losses quickly and say, "Hey! I got out. It didn't cost me much. I'm feeling pretty good."

Of course you could look at it like many inexperienced investors might: "That cost me something. I want revenge on the market. I will never forget that loss."

People are irrationally pained by the notion of loss. They are pained even more by these wide differences of perspective about loss.

These different points of view have a lot to do with your previous experiences, the kind of life that you have led, your mentors, and so on. For example, for some people real estate looks real, and it does have the word right in it—*real*. And as an uncle of Faulkner's said to him when he was young, "Buy land, they're not making any more of it." Those early messages make investing and trading as adults, seem very wise, even if they are not actually smart rules for making money.

I don't think there is anyone alive who would unilaterally accept real estate as a sound buy-and-hold investment with no downside. We all know better now.

## Old School Is Not New School

Early on Faulkner traded commodities and currencies making a tidy sum of profit. He called his mother and father one day to tell them about his success and mentioned the dollar profit. His mother quickly said, "You take that money and put it in the bank right now."

In his parents' world, that was a much safer place. You might think, "Banks? I wouldn't put it in a bank. It wouldn't be safe there."

That was Faulkner's thought too.

Let's face it. There have been a number of massive changes in the way people view the world. Before the Depression era people did not travel very much. Most people stayed in one place their entire lives, but now over 50 percent of the country is mobile to new areas every five years. That is a massive change in lifestyle for modern man.

Further, our grandparents had direct experiences. If you think about it, a majority of people's experiences are now virtual and or remote. Meaning if you are looking at a stock price, it's remote from you, it's abstract, and it's not like you're actually trading the physical shares. Who has stock certificates today? These changes have affected our current ideas, images, and beliefs.

Many feel these changes are positive with no unintended consequences. Faulkner sees it very differently.

He argues against the idea that there has been a democratization of the stock market. There have been investments made on behalf of people without their knowledge. Very often people don't know what they are invested in through their pension funds and mutual funds. In terms of pension funds, many of these operations enrich the fund managers more than they enrich the pensioners. It is a huge problem with mutual funds too. Mutual funds deliver no returns for a decade and still make billions for their owners. The system is backwards.

## Find the Essence

If you look around today, everything is about money. You cannot return to nature without paying for the space to pitch your tent. You cannot hunt for food without paying for the license to hunt (or fish). Money is our lifeblood, a stream running through our culture. It's fundamental. A basic competence at making money is not a luxury.

If you divide investing and trading into different categories: real estate, stocks, commodities, futures, ETFs, alternative assets, and so on, how are you going to evaluate them? Are you going to go into the fundamental details? Like a Jim Rogers or Warren Buffet? Are you going to tear the company balance sheet apart and digest arcane balance sheet details? Find out who's the CEO? What's the price-earnings ratio?

That's the old way.

You can go in another direction. You can abstract up and say, "What do all these things have in common?" Meaning, what do markets all have in common? Trend followers see price as the big differentiator, the element they have in common. It is a distinct way of thinking.

When you move into the world of trend followers there are no stories (a common theme across all chapters). Trend followers do not care about the company CEO's marriage or family life before buying a stock. They are not interested in outside factors. Just give them the price data.

This does not sit well with some newcomers and critics. They say, "Okay, I don't know the causative story, so I'm not going to indulge my mind in that." They just put the horse blinders onto this new way of trend thinking.

Years ago Faulkner saw Ed Seykota at a conference (he appears again) trying to win over converts. Seykota told attendees, "This market has the property of going up." Faulkner thought, "Wow, is this guy being careful with his language. He's not introducing any story, even in his own head." Whereas, everyone else wanted to know "why"—"why is it going up?" Faulkner saw Seykota's subtleness and depth, which was a great lesson.

Successful trend following trading is about developing a belief deep in your belly that you are part of a larger system. The world is not your world. You exist in a flowing river, and figuring out how you can navigate that flow is the much bigger question to answer versus how do you control it—because you can't.

There is no mastering the uncontrollable, but you don't have to control anything, except your downside, to make serious money.

## Follow the Leader

Faulkner paints a great picture of "now": Trend followers exist in the moment of now. Like a Mobius loop, the last principle circles back to the first one: "No one can predict the future." Nor can anyone get hints or messages from there because there's no there, there. When the "not yet now" happens, it's not the future, it's now. That is, until it's yesterday—an unreliable collection of memories only experienced . . . now. With only now, there's no room for stories, reasons, historical precedence, or other ideas requiring a past and future as if they are actual places instead of mental ideas we created. All of our would-bes, could-bes, should-bes, and should-of-beens are found in these imagined pasts and hoped for futures. In fact, some emotions require a disappointing past (regret) or an unfulfilled future (greed). When you realize there is only now, these would-a, could-a, should-as and their accompanying emotions become easier to set aside, making it possible to see what actually is . . . now. "There is only now" also focuses the mind. This moment is all there is. Our imperfect understanding of it is all we get. Act now . . . or not . . . in the next moment (of now), it's all there is, and different from the previous now in unpredictable ways, and our imperfect understanding of it is all we get.

In this world, clarity and simplicity are very highly valued, in thought and in action. This might seem quite Zen-like or mystical, but it's not. It was first recognized by the western psychologist Mihaly Csikszentmihalyi as "flow"—being so totally in an activity that one forgets oneself. It often happens when we fall in love with something or someone, or when we're playing a favorite sport or a musical instrument. It can also happen in so-called mindless activities, like washing the car, and suddenly your mind fills with new ideas.

What's finally so fascinating about this is whether you believe it or not, there is only *now*.

# Chapter Twelve

# Sing the Whipsaw Song

YOU MAY HAVE NOTICED A RECURRING NAME IN THE chapters of *The Little Book of Trading*. I had no plans to mention Ed Seykota in five chapters of this book—it just happened. During my research process, the traders kept bringing up Seykota's name, over and over again.

For those unfamiliar, Seykota was originally profiled in the classic book *Market Wizards*, and is considered one of the legendary trend following traders of our time. He has influenced a tremendous number of traders—far more than are mentioned in this book.

My path first crossed with Seykota in 2001. He invited me to the U. S. Virgin Islands. The time spent with Seykota, and the ensuing phone conversations and e-mails over the years, have become some of my most influential trend following trading lessons. I would not be writing this book and passing along wisdom without Seykota's generosity and early mentoring.

While it was a pleasant surprise to see Seykota woven throughout the lives of other great traders, in this very small world of ours it should have not been terribly unexpected. When you decide you want the chance at making the big money, when you decide that you really are serious, there are only so many living original sources around who are willing to share. Seykota is one.

And unlike this book, which is filled with words, albeit words that I consider very important to your future financial success, Seykota perhaps does an even better job of getting the trend following point across in his video on YouTube. It's actually a music video of trend following—the only one that exists so far. It is a video that could only come out of the mind of Ed Seykota. To give you a feel for the song before you see the video, Seykota allowed his lyrics to be republished here. It is called *The Whipsaw Song*.

What does *whipsaw* mean? It is a condition where a market price heads in one direction, but then is followed quickly by a movement in the opposite direction. The term derives from the push and pull action used by lumberjacks to cut wood with a type of saw that has the same name.

*The Whipsaw Song* is to the tune of *The Crawdad Song*, a traditional bluegrass tune in the key of A.

Chorus:
You get a whip and I get a saw, honey
You get a whip and I get a saw, babe
You get a whip and I get a saw
**One good trend pays for 'em all.**
Honey, trader, ba-by mine.

Banjo (Ride Your Winners):
What do we do when we catch a trend,
    honey . . . etc.
**We ride that trend right to the end.**

Mandolin (Cut Your Losses):
What do we do when we show a loss,
    honey . . . etc.
**We give that dag-gone loss a toss.**

Fiddle (Manage Your Risk):
How do we know when our risk is right,
    honey . . . etc.
**We make a lot of money and we sleep
    at night.**

Guitar (Use Stops):
What do we do when the price breaks through,
    honey . . . etc.
**Our stops are in so there's nothing to do.**

Bass (Stick to the System):
What do we do when a drawdown comes,
    honey
What do we do when it gets real big, babe
What do we do when it's even bigger . . .
**We stick to the plan and pull the trigger.**

Banjo (File the News):
What do we do with a hot news flash,
    honey . . . etc.
**We stash that flash right in the trash.**

Now go watch the video at www.seykota.com.

## Step Up or Step Down

Now what? You have a choice to make. You can either go down the path of becoming a trend following trader, becoming the next Larry Hite or Kevin Bruce, or you can invest your money with a trend following trader. That's it. The choices are clear. You either do or not do. It's very black or white.

Of course, you can always buy and hold some *top* mutual fund and hope that strategy will give you enough money to retire on by the time you get there or before another buy-and-hope market collapse of minus 50 percent. Forget that. The case has been laid out here for the benefits of trend following trading. The strategies of winners have been shown to give you confidence. Now it's up to you to decide what you want to be when you grow up.

I enjoyed researching and writing *The Little Book of Trading*. It has been a much different experience and challenge as compared to my prior books. My other books (see www.trendfollowing.com) were perhaps less accessible for the average reader. I hope *The Little Book of Trading* fills the void for those searching for something different. Good luck and feel free to contact me at www.covel.com.

# Appendix A
# Getting Technical

~

## *What is Capitalism Distribution?*\*

THE STOCK MARKET YIELDS A MINORITY OF VERY LARGE winners, a majority of below average returns, and a larger than expected number of dramatic losers. This phenomenon is Capitalism Distribution, and it can be observed in virtually any market, on any continent, across any decade. Capitalism is brutal, lumpy, and winner-take-all.

In Chapter 10, we met Eric Crittenden and Cole Wilcox. The database they use to find winning stocks covers

\*Adapted from "The Capitalism Distribution: Observations of Individual Common Stock Returns, 1983–2006," a research paper by Eric Crittenden and Cole Wilcox. Used with permission.

**Exhibit A.1   Total Lifetime Returns for Russell 3000 Stocks, 1983–2006**

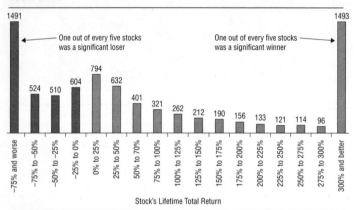

*Source:* Adapted from Table 1 in "The Capitalism Distribution: Observations of Individual Common Stock Returns, 1983–2006," a research paper by Eric Crittenden and Cole Wilcox. Used with permission.

all common stocks that traded on the NYSE, AMEX, and NASDAQ since 1983, including delisted stocks. Stock and index returns were calculated on a total return basis (dividends reinvested). Dynamic point-in-time liquidity filters were used to limit the universe to the approximately 8,000 (due to index reconstitution, delisting, mergers, etc.) stocks that would have qualified for membership in the Russell 3000 at some point in their lifetime. The Russell 3000 Index measures the performance of the largest 3,000 U.S. companies representing approximately 98 percent of the investable U.S. equity market. (See Exhibit A.1.)

**Exhibit A.2    Compounded Annual Return, 1991–2008**

| | |
|---|---|
| If you miss the worst 25% | 26% |
| If you miss the worst 10% | 16% |
| If you miss the worst 5% | 12% |
| All Russell 3000 stocks | 8% |
| If you miss the best 5% | −1% |
| If you miss the best 10% | −5% |
| If you miss the best 25% | −15% |

An investor who owned 95 percent of all stocks, but who missed the 5 percent best performing each year, would have lost money from 1991 to 2008. Alternatively, an investor who owned 90 percent of all stocks and managed to avoid the 10 percent worst performing would have doubled the market's compounded annual return (see Exhibit A.2). Clearly, a small minority of very strong and very weak stocks have a disproportionate impact on results.

Money management is crucial to investment success. A positive average return (mathematical expectancy) is not enough. Consider a simple coin flip analogy. Heads you win 200 percent, tails you lose 100 percent (not unlike an investment in a single stock). This equates to a 2:1 win/loss ratio and a 50 percent win rate, which yields an average return of +50 percent per coin flip. However, to achieve this +50 percent average return, you'd have to bet everything on each coin flip. In doing so, you'd go broke, with certainty, the first time you experience a loss. How can you have a positive average return and go broke?

If you start with $100 and enjoy a 200 percent return you'll have $300. If you then suffer a –100 percent loss you'll have $0. But your average return will be +50 percent (200% – 100%)/2 = +50%.

How much should you bet per coin flip? In the case of this coin flip analogy, risking 25 percent on each flip results in the highest compounded return over time. Risking more than this yields lower returns, higher volatility, and deeper drawdowns in equity. Risking more than 50 percent (over-betting) results in losses, despite having

**Exhibit A.3    Watch Your Losses—10:1 Win/Loss Ratio**

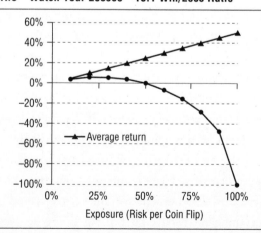

**Exhibit A.4    Compound Return Using 10:1 Win/Loss Ratio**

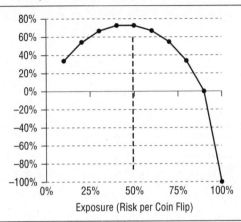

a favorable bet with a positive average return. Some refer to this phenomenon as *volatility gremlins* or *variance drain*. Take a look at Exhibit A.3.

Compounding is more sensitive to losses than to gains. Even if the amount won on a coin flip is 10 times greater than the amount lost, there is no benefit to risking more than 50 percent per flip. As you can see from Exhibit A.4, that would be over-betting.

Readers interested in this concept should refer to the works of Ralph Vince, Ed Thorp, David Druz, and Ed Seykota.

# Appendix B
# Fund Performance Data

~

THE TRADERS AND FUNDS I'VE TALKED ABOUT IN THIS book are a big deal, and they're making it big by sticking to trend following. But maybe you need more proof. Consider these performance numbers. They show that trend following excels in the long run. Even if you thought every word of this book was complete bull, try explaining these performance numbers to me.

*Note:* All tables show composite monthly and annual rates of return (%) net of all fees.

## Chadwick Investment Group

| Year | Jan | Feb | Mar | Apr | May | Jun | Jul | Aug | Sep | Oct | Nov | Dec | YTD |
|------|-----|-----|-----|-----|-----|-----|-----|-----|-----|-----|-----|-----|-----|
| 2010 | -6.83 | -2.37 | 6.32 | -6.06 | 15.38 | -7.50 | 6.67 | 8.00 | 12.30 | 14.02 | -9.52 | 7.00 | 38.47 |
| 2009 | -1.77 | -4.94 | -6.98 | -1.49 | 11.15 | -2.98 | -4.89 | 8.25 | 0.68 | -6.47 | 10.68 | -16.34 | -17.17 |
| 2008 | 2.79 | 15.58 | -0.34 | 1.06 | 7.41 | 12.65 | -11.15 | 0.11 | 9.39 | 21.05 | 4.93 | 2.05 | 82.60 |
| 2007 | | | | | | 7.00 | 0.73 | -1.61 | 7.58 | 3.08 | -0.34 | 0.46 | 17.74 |

*Source:* www.iasg.com/groups/group/chadwick-investment-group/program/diversified-trend-following.

## Drury Capital

| Year | Jan | Feb | Mar | Apr | May | Jun | Jul | Aug | Sep | Oct | Nov | Dec | YTD |
|------|------|------|------|------|------|------|------|------|------|------|------|------|------|
| 2010 | −6.25 | −1.35 | 6.12 | 0.38 | −7.87 | 0.18 | −4.88 | 2.66 | 4.19 | 4.12 | −4.19 | 9.06 | 0.65 |
| 2009 | −1.82 | 2.10 | −3.64 | −2.72 | 1.82 | −0.23 | 6.57 | 2.67 | 1.54 | −3.53 | 6.48 | 0.09 | 9.04 |
| 2008 | 6.78 | 11.17 | −8.45 | −5.44 | 7.44 | 6.63 | −9.45 | 1.92 | 16.95 | 23.37 | 6.56 | 5.15 | 75.65 |
| 2007 | 3.33 | −3.51 | 0.08 | 3.21 | 3.39 | 7.79 | −5.60 | −5.31 | 2.93 | −0.67 | 3.56 | −3.29 | 5.05 |
| 2006 | −0.51 | −0.69 | 0.37 | 2.38 | −2.15 | −1.28 | −6.44 | −1.22 | 0.91 | −4.47 | −6.34 | 3.38 | −15.40 |
| 2005 | −2.34 | −4.57 | 0.27 | −5.56 | −4.02 | −2.42 | −0.65 | 1.83 | 1.15 | 0.95 | 7.85 | −2.78 | −10.47 |
| 2004 | 2.45 | 11.09 | 2.33 | −6.97 | −6.06 | −1.21 | −0.45 | −5.85 | 7.78 | −1.13 | 7.20 | −0.36 | 7.27 |
| 2003 | 7.76 | 6.94 | −6.32 | −4.10 | 9.42 | −6.35 | −4.41 | −0.87 | 4.17 | 13.80 | −1.03 | 6.64 | 25.77 |
| 2002 | 0.52 | −1.32 | −2.05 | −3.68 | −5.13 | 11.62 | 4.82 | 3.75 | 4.35 | −9.42 | −5.97 | 10.19 | 5.55 |
| 2001 | −6.20 | 4.95 | 15.48 | −4.19 | 2.41 | 4.97 | −3.66 | 2.03 | 6.23 | 3.82 | −9.34 | 4.82 | 20.62 |
| 2000 | −5.58 | 0.35 | −1.59 | 11.91 | 1.14 | −4.41 | 1.49 | 4.92 | −1.70 | 3.26 | 6.33 | −0.12 | 15.80 |
| 1999 | 0.06 | 6.05 | −2.82 | 4.46 | −5.56 | −0.36 | −4.43 | 8.54 | −3.59 | −1.24 | 5.20 | 4.88 | 10.46 |
| 1998 | 7.84 | 6.11 | 6.60 | −5.46 | 7.78 | 2.20 | −1.38 | 19.34 | −5.22 | −2.74 | 4.25 | 2.46 | 47.21 |
| 1997 | | | | | −4.57 | 14.98 | 12.49 | −2.12 | −2.08 | −9.35 | 17.34 | 3.64 | 30.42 |

Source: www.iasg.com/groups/group/drury-capital/program/diversified-trend-following-program.

**Mulvaney Capital Management**

| Year | Jan | Feb | Mar | Apr | May | Jun | Jul | Aug | Sep | Oct | Nov | Dec | YTD |
|---|---|---|---|---|---|---|---|---|---|---|---|---|---|
| 2010 | -3.84 | -7.15 | -5.15 | 2.02 | -8.77 | 0.53 | -12.03 | 14.59 | 16.46 | 22.29 | -5.36 | 25.30 | 34.90 |
| 2009 | 1.60 | -0.03 | -3.36 | -5.51 | -1.30 | -6.81 | -0.53 | 10.85 | 1.32 | -7.86 | 10.70 | -3.19 | -5.89 |
| 2008 | 21.65 | 28.86 | -7.96 | -8.58 | 5.35 | 8.51 | -18.78 | -6.73 | 11.58 | 45.49 | 6.97 | 5.30 | 108.87 |
| 2007 | 0.56 | -5.18 | -8.82 | 2.59 | 4.70 | 4.85 | -16.89 | -19.40 | 3.92 | 13.72 | -8.59 | 8.47 | -23.14 |
| 2006 | 11.09 | -2.70 | 13.05 | 11.46 | -4.27 | -6.10 | -5.20 | 1.95 | 1.00 | -0.13 | 0.56 | 1.60 | 21.94 |
| 2005 | -4.28 | 0.54 | 2.30 | -9.28 | -4.08 | 5.32 | 6.62 | 2.78 | 13.57 | -5.64 | 15.27 | 8.35 | 32.34 |
| 2004 | 4.19 | 8.45 | 2.37 | -11.50 | -6.99 | -0.73 | -0.41 | -6.21 | 7.76 | 0.76 | 9.63 | -4.94 | -0.10 |
| 2003 | 13.20 | 7.22 | -12.83 | 1.45 | 7.64 | -7.61 | -6.33 | 0.07 | 6.66 | 15.32 | -0.27 | 5.35 | 29.30 |
| 2002 | 0.00 | 0.00 | -7.52 | 1.55 | 6.75 | 7.38 | 5.95 | 5.44 | 5.13 | -7.73 | -5.08 | 7.80 | 19.37 |
| 2001 | -9.62 | 18.76 | 13.46 | -15.25 | -0.66 | 5.39 | -1.26 | 0.00 | 0.00 | 0.00 | 0.00 | 0.00 | 6.69 |
| 2000 | -5.02 | 2.52 | -8.40 | -0.27 | 6.97 | 1.55 | -1.25 | 12.68 | -4.36 | 1.96 | 9.05 | 8.90 | 24.51 |
| 1999 | | | | | -0.29 | -0.14 | -2.22 | 2.13 | -4.81 | -4.80 | 7.01 | 4.84 | 1.09 |

*Source:* www.iasg.com/groups/group/mulvaney-capital-management/program/global-diversified-program.

## Sunrise Capital Partners

| Year | Jan | Feb | Mar | Apr | May | Jun | Jul | Aug | Sep | Oct | Nov | Dec | YTD |
|------|------|------|------|------|-------|------|------|-------|------|------|-------|------|------|
| 2010 | −4.4 | −0.4 | 2.3 | −0.4 | −12.3 | −0.6 | −3.4 | 1.7 | 3.7 | 5.6 | −1.6 | −1.9 | −5.8 |
| 2009 | −1.9 | −0.4 | −2.0 | −1.6 | 3.1 | −0.2 | 2.2 | 2.9 | 0.7 | −0.6 | 5.0 | 1.3 | 5.2 |
| 2008 | 6.6 | 9.5 | −1.3 | −2.8 | 2.5 | 2.6 | −4.1 | −2.1 | 2.4 | 12.9 | 4.2 | 2.3 | 34.8 |
| 2007 | 3.4 | −2.7 | −5.0 | 6.0 | 3.4 | 1.8 | −5.2 | −12.6 | 6.9 | 8.5 | 2.2 | 2.4 | 7.2 |
| 2006 | −0.7 | 0.1 | 3.1 | 2.9 | 0.8 | −1.0 | −3.4 | −1.0 | 0.4 | 3.3 | 1.4 | 1.3 | 8.4 |
| 2005 | −6.9 | 0.2 | −0.8 | −1.6 | 0.0 | 1.2 | −2.1 | −0.2 | −0.3 | 0.5 | 7.0 | 1.3 | −2.1 |
| 2004 | 1.3 | 7.5 | 1.7 | −3.9 | −1.9 | −1.8 | −2.1 | −4.8 | 0.7 | 3.9 | 5.0 | 9.4 | 6.3 |
| 2003 | 9.5 | 4.8 | −6.4 | 0.4 | 6.5 | −4.0 | −2.3 | 0.3 | −3.1 | 6.0 | −0.3 | 8.8 | 20.8 |
| 2002 | −0.4 | −3.8 | −0.1 | 0.4 | 5.3 | 11.7 | 2.0 | 0.8 | 5.9 | −4.3 | −5.7 | 3.0 | 21.1 |
| 2001 | −0.3 | 3.7 | 7.6 | −5.4 | 3.3 | −0.6 | −2.5 | 2.8 | 8.0 | 6.4 | −10.6 | 7.8 | 14.6 |
| 2000 | 4.4 | −3.2 | −1.0 | −4.4 | −1.0 | −0.1 | 0.7 | 3.9 | −1.6 | 1.7 | 5.8 | −2.1 | 12.9 |
| 1999 | −0.4 | 5.7 | −1.1 | 4.2 | −0.8 | 2.8 | −1.7 | 0.2 | 0.5 | −4.0 | 5.1 | 2.9 | 8.1 |
| 1998 | 1.5 | 3.5 | 2.8 | 1.7 | 2.6 | 3.3 | −0.5 | 8.8 | 3.5 | −1.3 | −5.0 | 2.6 | 26.1 |
| 1997 | 5.2 | 8.9 | 1.6 | −0.3 | 4.5 | −3.0 | 6.4 | −3.1 | −1.3 | −1.1 | 1.9 | 3.0 | 23.7 |
| 1996 | 0.5 | −5.8 | 4.5 | 9.3 | 0.1 | −0.6 | −0.7 | −0.5 | 1.1 | 6.8 | 1.2 | 3.0 | 19.8 |

*Source*: www.sunrisecapital.com.

## Tactical Investment Management Corporation

| Year | Jan | Feb | Mar | Apr | May | Jun | Jul | Aug | Sep | Oct | Nov | Dec | YTD |
|------|------|------|------|------|------|------|------|------|------|------|------|------|------|
| 2010 | -1.63 | -3.23 | 4.88 | 2.26 | -2.40 | 3.24 | -0.54 | -3.65 | 19.98 | 18.27 | 9.23 | 10.55 | 68.90 |
| 2009 | 0.30 | -1.12 | -8.39 | -2.65 | 15.67 | -3.40 | 5.33 | 10.29 | -1.99 | -1.49 | 10.46 | -1.98 | 20.00 |
| 2008 | 8.09 | 21.39 | -7.18 | 0.14 | 2.05 | 6.78 | -12.30 | -1.64 | -1.15 | 26.62 | 1.38 | 1.98 | 48.35 |
| 2007 | -6.33 | -1.68 | -7.15 | 8.58 | -0.61 | 6.76 | -1.66 | -10.49 | 26.03 | 3.69 | -7.52 | 1.91 | 6.84 |
| 2006 | 16.31 | -6.10 | 6.94 | 15.83 | 1.00 | -2.61 | -10.06 | 4.52 | -4.15 | -0.28 | 8.02 | -3.79 | 24.26 |
| 2005 | -4.20 | 1.12 | -3.78 | -3.03 | 4.16 | -0.47 | -3.80 | 6.90 | 0.71 | -4.01 | 9.14 | 5.22 | 6.98 |
| 2004 | 4.51 | 14.38 | 1.44 | -18.94 | -7.83 | -7.31 | 6.49 | -3.17 | 5.98 | 4.00 | 12.75 | 0.39 | 8.04 |
| 2003 | 10.47 | 9.08 | -7.41 | 4.31 | 6.11 | -6.42 | -7.00 | 0.34 | 1.71 | 12.69 | -2.04 | 6.75 | 29.26 |
| 2002 | -5.52 | 0.90 | -0.43 | -3.55 | 9.82 | 9.78 | 3.65 | 4.48 | 3.59 | -3.01 | 2.27 | 9.58 | 34.58 |
| 2001 | -1.79 | 2.46 | 13.89 | -7.74 | 3.04 | 3.61 | -3.37 | 1.99 | 5.29 | 8.13 | -9.62 | 1.55 | 16.26 |
| 2000 | 3.82 | -0.18 | -4.05 | 1.34 | 8.37 | -3.59 | -1.20 | 3.46 | -1.01 | 4.57 | 9.67 | 8.64 | 32.74 |
| 1999 | -12.38 | 1.98 | -8.81 | 4.56 | -9.82 | -1.91 | 0.93 | 2.77 | 5.24 | -14.95 | 2.85 | 3.21 | -25.74 |
| 1998 | -1.63 | -4.06 | -2.24 | -4.47 | 3.80 | 5.11 | -0.97 | 18.34 | -1.82 | -1.94 | -6.00 | 11.03 | 13.23 |
| 1997 | 10.50 | 9.17 | -1.09 | -5.72 | 8.00 | -11.57 | 14.29 | 4.03 | 4.68 | -2.06 | 0.08 | 5.10 | 37.75 |
| 1996 | -8.81 | -4.21 | 4.85 | 32.24 | -7.49 | 2.68 | -8.39 | 4.68 | 9.63 | 10.13 | 9.17 | -6.43 | 36.07 |

| Year | | | | | | | | | | | | | |
|---|---|---|---|---|---|---|---|---|---|---|---|---|---|
| 1995 | -7.78 | 2.33 | 16.84 | 6.61 | 12.27 | 2.46 | -8.18 | -5.91 | -3.06 | 2.17 | 6.47 | 34.82 | 66.06 |
| 1994 | -14.33 | -14.53 | -0.68 | 0.16 | 10.39 | 0.82 | -5.71 | -8.34 | 4.15 | 3.82 | 16.43 | 2.94 | -9.20 |
| 1993 | 0.87 | 15.21 | -7.68 | -0.10 | 6.00 | 6.20 | 17.40 | 5.75 | -6.69 | -4.53 | 5.75 | 4.93 | 48.08 |
| 1992 | -6.55 | -10.29 | -1.80 | 12.15 | -2.29 | 17.82 | 17.05 | 7.17 | -0.22 | -5.10 | 2.98 | -6.34 | 21.78 |
| 1991 | -19.09 | -4.71 | 4.69 | -6.51 | -5.08 | 8.29 | -5.96 | -10.11 | 4.25 | 2.62 | -1.95 | 27.58 | -12.26 |
| 1990 | 6.01 | 7.62 | 7.67 | 9.56 | -9.23 | 5.49 | 16.26 | 10.78 | 18.20 | 3.52 | 1.29 | -4.49 | 96.46 |
| 1989 | 1.30 | -9.37 | 3.74 | -10.69 | 20.27 | -11.22 | 3.85 | -11.94 | -1.46 | -26.02 | 3.81 | 11.39 | -29.98 |
| 1988 | -4.58 | 4.97 | -11.75 | -21.37 | 22.55 | 71.56 | -10.03 | 3.71 | 1.50 | -3.14 | 5.68 | 5.06 | 48.83 |
| 1987 | -0.65 | -5.08 | -0.72 | 63.28 | 9.50 | -6.93 | 10.98 | -10.46 | 0.75 | -13.38 | 13.89 | 12.05 | 72.39 |
| 1986 | 1.93 | 33.74 | 0.23 | -11.98 | -4.52 | -15.24 | 4.03 | 2.49 | -19.08 | -19.45 | -6.30 | 8.19 | -31.43 |
| 1985 | -1.39 | -2.95 | 1.10 | -1.44 | -1.81 | -7.37 | 28.33 | 2.76 | -11.68 | 14.37 | -0.81 | -6.61 | 7.03 |
| 1984 | -3.47 | -8.69 | -0.79 | -4.05 | 12.41 | -1.71 | 16.59 | -4.68 | 2.62 | -4.94 | -3.87 | 3.81 | 0.30 |
| 1983 | 5.13 | 2.06 | -6.92 | -0.84 | 18.65 | -18.61 | 6.02 | 30.98 | -7.11 | 5.73 | -11.36 | 3.23 | 19.34 |
| 1982 | 7.51 | 4.74 | 7.36 | -0.34 | 1.47 | 5.74 | -3.73 | 17.39 | 14.70 | -8.39 | -4.44 | -11.16 | 30.32 |
| 1981 | | | | | | | -2.63 | 8.22 | -2.06 | -4.20 | 15.00 | 2.42 | 16.46 |

*Source:* www.tacticalnet.com

## Winton Capital Management

| Year | Jan | Feb | Mar | Apr | May | Jun | Jul | Aug | Sep | Oct | Nov | Dec | YTD |
|---|---|---|---|---|---|---|---|---|---|---|---|---|---|
| 2010 | -2.64 | 2.33 | 4.91 | 1.75 | -1.01 | 1.47 | -2.78 | 4.78 | 0.94 | 2.51 | -2.01 | 3.75 | 14.47 |
| 2009 | 0.99 | -0.21 | -1.64 | -3.01 | -2.03 | -1.26 | -1.52 | 0.32 | 2.85 | -1.59 | 5.12 | -2.45 | -4.64 |
| 2008 | 3.85 | 7.95 | -0.66 | -0.99 | 1.99 | 5.06 | -4.63 | -3.00 | -0.41 | 3.73 | 4.97 | 2.10 | 21.01 |
| 2007 | 3.86 | -5.93 | -3.95 | 6.46 | 5.05 | 1.91 | -1.18 | -0.88 | 6.99 | 2.52 | 2.42 | 0.24 | 17.97 |
| 2006 | 4.20 | -2.58 | 4.01 | 5.66 | -2.94 | -1.17 | -0.47 | 4.54 | -1.10 | 1.48 | 3.24 | 2.14 | 17.84 |
| 2005 | -5.38 | 6.58 | 4.64 | -4.21 | 6.62 | 3.13 | -1.85 | 7.63 | -6.17 | -2.95 | 7.32 | -4.37 | 9.73 |
| 2004 | 2.72 | 11.56 | -0.80 | -8.62 | 0.28 | -2.96 | 1.33 | 3.09 | 5.14 | 4.03 | 6.37 | -0.19 | 22.62 |
| 2003 | 5.95 | 11.95 | -10.80 | 2.45 | 10.19 | -5.20 | -0.68 | 0.62 | 0.26 | 4.72 | -2.48 | 10.27 | 27.76 |
| 2002 | -10.13 | -6.04 | 12.62 | -3.76 | -3.96 | 7.95 | 4.71 | 6.04 | 7.63 | -7.96 | -0.69 | 14.16 | 18.33 |
| 2001 | 4.38 | 0.56 | 7.09 | -5.31 | -2.61 | -2.66 | 0.66 | 0.56 | 4.64 | 13.75 | -7.10 | -5.15 | 7.12 |
| 2000 | -3.96 | 1.72 | -3.28 | 2.06 | -0.26 | -1.27 | -4.58 | 3.23 | -7.76 | 2.09 | 7.33 | 16.81 | 10.43 |
| 1999 | -1.38 | 3.61 | -3.98 | 10.51 | -8.39 | 5.29 | -2.01 | -3.47 | -0.17 | -6.20 | 13.93 | 9.04 | 15.08 |
| 1998 | 1.50 | 3.27 | 7.38 | -1.63 | 8.53 | 2.97 | 1.51 | 10.99 | 4.51 | -5.70 | 1.15 | 9.50 | 52.17 |
| 1997 | | | | | | | | | | -12.97 | 9.96 | 8.14 | 3.49 |

Source: www.iasg.com/groups/group/winton-capital-management/program/diversified.

# Glossary of Key Terms

**Bollinger Bands**   A technical analysis tool consisting of three bands drawn around a market price. The middle band measures the intermediate-term trend, usually a moving average, and serves as a base for the upper band and lower band. The interval between the upper and lower bands and the middle band is determined by volatility, typically the standard deviation of the same data that were used for the average. Developed by trader John Bollinger.

**channel breakout**   Another term used to describe Bollinger Bands, or close approximations of Bollinger Bands.

**Commodity Futures Trading Commission (CFTC)**
The U.S. federal regulatory agency for the futures industry, first established in 1974.

**commodity trading advisor (CTA)**   An individual or organization that is paid to directly or indirectly advise others on the buying and selling of futures contracts. Must be registered with the CFTC and NFA.

**compound interest**   Interest that accrues on initial principal. It also accrues on accumulated interest of principal.

**disclosure document**   The document that CTAs must supply when soliciting customers. It typically contains disclosure statements, performance records, information on business background and trading methodology, and advisory agreement papers.

**drawdown**   The peak-to-trough measurement in both time and money of an account's losing period. See also **peak-to-trough**.

**efficient market hypothesis (EMH)**   The efficient market hypothesis states that all available information is known to investors and or traders, hence their decisions are deemed rational. Trend followers believe just the opposite.

**exchange traded fund (ETF)**   A fund traded on stock exchanges not unlike a stock (i.e., they have a symbol like stocks). ETFs can consist of stocks, bonds, futures, currencies, and so on. ETFs can employ many different types of strategies. Many ETFs attempt to emulate futures contracts.

**hedger**   A hedger is a person who typically takes a position in one market in an attempt to offset exposure in some opposite position.

**fat tail**   In the normal distribution of portfolio returns, the far ends of the bell curve are called *tails*. The term is used to describe a deviation from a statistical normal distribution. Trend following trading routinely wins by capturing extreme and unforeseen events—the fat tails (otherwise known as the 100-year floods).

**fundamental analysis**   A form of market analysis that attempts to divine market direction through study of all factors perceived to affect supply and demand. These could include analysis of the Federal Reserve, crop reports, OPEC, P/E ratios, and so on.

**futures (or futures contract)**   An agreement to buy or sell a particular financial instrument at a predetermined price. Futures contracts detail the quality and quantity of the underlying market. They are standardized and traded on futures exchanges (such as CME Group).

**managed account**   An arrangement by which the owner of an account gives written power of attorney to a CTA to buy and sell without prior approval of the account owner. Also called discretionary account.

**mechanical trading**   A trading approach in which buy and sell signals are automated through computing technology. Trend following is regularly made mechanical.

**money manager**   An individual or organization that allocates assets to CTAs and manages the allocations on behalf of investors. Generally registered as a CTA and CPO with the CFTC or as a registered investment adviser with the Securities and Exchange Commission.

**moving average**   An analysis tool that averages a market price over a set time period.

**peak-to-trough**   A drawdown measurement made from an account's all-time equity high to a low. The measurement typically is made on a month-end basis.

**rate of return**   The percentage of money gained or lost on an investment relative to the amount of money invested.

**speculator**    Speculators accept risk in futures markets, aiming to profit from price changes that hedgers are protecting against. Trend followers are speculators.

**standard deviation**    A statistical measure used to measure market volatility. Does not accurately quantify trend following since it penalizes upside volatility.

**technical analysis**    An approach to market analysis that examines patterns of price change, rates of change, and changes in volume of trading and open interest. This approach does not involve the use of fundamental market factors. Trend following is a form of technical analysis.

**track record**    The entire performance history of a trader (i.e., CTA).

**trading system**    A system that generates buy and sell signals for a trading strategy. Most successful trading systems are trend following based.

**trend**    The general direction, either upward or downward, in which prices may move.

**whipsaw**    A condition where a market price heads in one direction but then is followed quickly by a movement in the opposite direction.

# Author Disclaimer

———— ≈ ————

MICHAEL W. COVEL SERVES AS PRESIDENT OF TREND Following™, a privately owned research firm. His trend following books include *The Little Book of Trading* (2011), *Trend Commandments* (2011), *The Complete Turtle Trader* (2009, 2007), and *Trend Following* (2009, 2007, 2005, 2004). For more information about systemic trend following trading systems, please see www.trendfollowing.com and www.covel.com.

Data from various sources were used in the preparation of this book. The information is believed to be reliable, accurate, and appropriate, but is not guaranteed in any way. Performance track records included are on file with the United States government and can be obtained via the Freedom of Information Act. This book also contains the names of some companies and individuals used as examples of the strategies described, but none can be deemed recommendations to the book's readers. Strategies discussed in this text may be inappropriate for some investors, and you are urged to speak with a financial professional and carefully review any pertinent disclosures before implementing any investing or trading strategy. This book has been prepared solely for informational purposes, and is not an offer to buy or sell, or a solicitation to buy or sell, any security or instrument, or to participate in any particular trading strategy.

# Acknowledgments

---

I want to give special thanks to Michelle Sanks for her diligent work in helping to craft this book. "Going the extra mile" is her middle name. Rebecca Clear Dean, Robin Eggar, Martin Ehrlich, Jason Gerlach, Martin Klitzner, Eric Laing, and Matt Waz all helped to make this book possible. Thank you also goes to Cullen Roche of Pragmatic Capitalism (www.pragcap.com) for writing the Foreword. Lastly, a big thank you goes out to those who generously shared their wisdom with me—it is their *thinking* that forms the basis for this book:

Kevin Bruce (retired)

Michael Clarke—Clarke Capital Management, Inc. (www.clarkecap.com)

Eric Crittenden and Cole Wilcox—Longboard Asset
Management (www.longboard-am.com)

Gary Davis, Jack Forrest, and Rick Slaughter—Sunrise
Capital Partners (www.sunrisecapital.com)

Bernard Drury—Drury Capital Services
(www.drurycapital.com)

David Druz—Tactical Investment Management
Corporation (www.tacticalnet.com)

Charles Faulkner—Influential Communications
(www.charlesfaulkner.com)

David Harding—Winton Capital Management
(www.wintoncapital.com)

Larry Hite—International Standard Asset
Management (www.isamfunds.com)

Paul Mulvaney—Mulvaney Capital Management
(www.mulvaneycapital.com)

Justin Vandergrift—Chadwick Investment Group
(www.chadwicktrading.com)